THE NAVAJO
CODE TALKERS

DORIS A. PAUL

Photo of lithograph of Navajo code talkers, by John Fabion, Fourth Marine Division, combat artist, Professor Emeritus, Chicago Art Institute. Reprinted by permission of the artist.

THE NAVAJO CODE TALKERS

DORIS A. PAUL

DORRANCE PUBLISHING CO., INC.

643 SMITHFIELD STREET, PITTSBURGH, PENNSYLVANIA 15222

ISBN # 0-8059-1870-1
Library of Congress Catalog Card Number: 73-79199
Printed in the United States of America

Fourteenth Printing

For information or to order additional books, please write:
Dorrance Publishing Co., Inc.
643 Smithfield Street
Pittsburgh, Pennsylvania 15222
U.S.A.

To my grandson
JEFFREY BENTON GRIER

CONTENTS

Page

ACKNOWLEDGEMENTS

It would be impossible to list everyone who has in some way contributed to the writing of this book; but here are the names of some, without whose help efforts would have been fruitless.

Heading the list is Lee Cannon, whose dedication to human rights and whose love of people led him to spearhead a ceremony at which the Navajo Code Talkers received belated recognition for their contribution to their country during World War II. Mr. Cannon served as liaison between the author and Navajo personnel and the Marine Corps, and was also a prime source of inspiration.

Grateful acknowledgement is due Philip Johnston, who conceived the idea of a code based on the Navajo language and who "sold" the idea to the Marines. Without his encouragement and wealth of information, the book could never have been written.

Special credit goes to Martin Link, curator of the Navajo Tribal Museum, who made available all the resources of the museum and who gave full cooperation during the preparation of the manuscript.

To Wilson B. Paul, heartiest thanks for his assistance in gathering information and his constant encouragement during the years the book was in the process, and to Margery Ellen, educator, who counseled with her mother during the writing of the manuscript.

An accolade to the wonderful Navajos in official positions on the reservation! The author particularly appreciates the cooperation of the Honorable Raymond Nakai, chairman of the Navajo Nation at the time of the author's initial visit to the reservation, Anthony Lincoln, then director of the Navajo Tribe, John Claw of the Office of Design and Development, and W. Dean Wilson, Tribal Judge.

The author is grateful to the many code talkers who shared experiences with her through interviews and through correspondence. Those who were able to give the most information about the code talker program and the utilization of the code in action in the Pacific are: Jimmy King, William McCabe, John Benally, Peter Sandoval, Sandy Burr, Teddy Draper, Carl Gorman, Albert Smith, John Brown, Jr., Paul Blatchford, Eugene Crawford, Samuel T. Holiday, Frank Thompson, Sam Silversmith and Ambrose Howard. She is grateful also to the many Anglo Marines who volunteered human interest stories about life with the Navajos in combat areas, as well as enlightening information as to the use of the code in action.

Acknowledgement is due personnel at Marine Corps Headquarters in Washington. The author particularly wishes to thank Colonel F. C. Caldwell, director of Marine Corps History, for valuable information from the archives, and Colonel Richard L. McDaniel of the Combat Pictorial Branch for photographs of the code talkers on duty in the Pacific area.

PROLOGUE

The hours were dark, after the vicious attack at Pearl Harbor on December 7, 1941. Japan had chosen a sinister and savage way in which to throw down the gauntlet. Those in high places in the government hastily took stock of our remaining resources. We had to protect Hawaii and the West Coast in some way, with what seemed to be a hopelessly crippled navy. We also had to establish a foothold in the Pacific to stave off the enemy. All this was the problem of the chiefs of staff and their aides.

The people of this country rallied; volunteers flocked to the colors; and slowly, cautiously we sailed, in remnants of the fleet, toward Japanese-held territory.

A civil engineer in Los Angeles, Philip Johnston, suggested to the Marines a plan to prevent communications from being decoded by the highly-trained, ingenious Japanese cryptographers. This book tells the story: the acceptance of the plan to employ a code based on the Navajo tongue, following a protracted period of weighing it in the balances, and the part the code eventually played in confusing the enemy and forcing him to surrender.

The famed code talkers were the descendants of the men and women, who, less than eighty years before, had been driven from their homes among the four sacred mountains of Navajo country—driven like cattle for three hundred miles to Fort Sumner, a "concentration camp" for Indians—in what has come to be known as "the long walk." The code talkers were the descendants of these same men and women whose homes and crops were burned by Kit Carson and his men, and who, after four miserable years, were finally returned—to a scorched wilderness.

The code talkers represented a tribe so loyal to our country, in spite of their bitter heritage, that they poured out of the far reaches of the reservation in great numbers, carrying old muskets and hunting rifles, after hearing the news of the Pearl Harbor debacle. Asked recently why they fight the white man's wars, their chairman replied, "Because we are proud to be Americans!"

This, then, is a book about the brave, sometimes inscrutable Navajos, with the spotlight on the code talkers who transmitted countless messages during World War II in a language so foreign to the Japanese that not a syllable could be deciphered.

Chapter One

THE SECRET WEAPON

...Every syllable of my message came through.

Sometimes we had to crawl, had to run, had to lie partly submerged in a swamp or in a lagoon, or in the dead heat, pinned under fire. But there was no problem. We transmitted our messages under any and all conditions,

says a Navajo, who was a member of one of the first units of Navajo code talkers, and who became an instructor in the code both in camp and in the field.
He continues:

During their last dying efforts, the Japanese felt that if they could just get one more Marine, could crawl over a certain line, they'd do it. You might say they went out of their heads. They were ... shall we say ... desperate, and would do anything to prevent what the Marines finally came through with. They thought, "If this is the last thing I can do for the Emperor—to give my life—I'll do it!"
One night we held them down. If you so much as held up your head six inches you were gone, the fire was so intense. And then in the wee hours, with no relief on our side or theirs, there was a dead standstill. Anything—any sound from anywhere—called for fire. If there was any movement —the breaking of a little twig—maybe there would be a hundred shots there. You just sat or lay there, gun cocked. It must have gotten so that this one Japanese couldn't take it anymore. He got up and yelled and screamed at the top of his voice and dashed over our trench, swinging a long samurai sword. I imagine he was shot from 25 to 40 times before he fell.

There was a buddy with me in the trench. For four days we had had no relief . . . hardly anything to eat; but we had to stay on the line. I had a cord tied around my wrist and to my buddy's hand. If I pulled the string and he pulled back there in the dark, I knew he was still alive. But that Japanese cut him across the throat, clear through to the cords on the back of his neck with that long sword. He was still gasping through his windpipe. When he exhaled, blood gushed. And the sound of his trying to breathe was horrible. He died without help, of course. When the Jap struck, warm blood spattered all over my hand that was holding a microphone. I was calling [in code] for help. They tell me that in spite of what happened, every syllable of my message came through.

Such was the stamina of the men from the Navajo reservation, who served as communicators in the Pacific area during World War II.

Long before December 7, 1941, when the Japanese made their massive attempt to destroy the American navy at Pearl Harbor, the Navajos had heard about the war that was gaining frightening proportions across the Atlantic. Many asked their superintendents for the privilege of listening collectively (by loudspeakers) to radio reports about the progress of the conflict. They nicknamed Hitler "Mustache Smeller" and referred to Mussolini as "Big Gourd Chin." The Japanese were called many names among which were "Slant Eyes" and "Narrow Eyes."

On the third of June, 1940, the Navajo Tribal Council at Window Rock passed, by unanimous vote, the following resolution, signed by J. C. Morgan, chairman, and Howard Gorman, vice-chairman:

Whereas, the Navajo Tribal Council and the 50,000 people we represent, cannot fail to recognize the crisis now facing the world in the threat of foreign invasion and the destruction of the great liberties and benefits which we enjoy on the reservation, and

Whereas, there exists no purer concentration of Americanism than among the First Americans, and

Whereas, it has become common practice to attempt national destruction through the sowing of seeds of treachery among minority groups such as ours, and

Whereas, we hereby serve notice that any un-American movement among our people will be resented and dealt with severely, and

Now, Therefore, we resolve that the Navajo Indians stand ready as they did in 1918, to aid and defend our Government and its institutions against all subversive and armed conflict and pledge our loyalty to the system which recognizes minority rights and a way of life that has placed us among the greatest people of our race.

At the outbreak of the war, the Navajos were isolated to the degree that only a comparatively small number had ever ventured off the reservation.

Only a pitifully small ratio of the children of the tribe were in attendance at mission schools or government boarding schools. Fortunately for the role the more intelligent and apt students were to play eventually in the pursuit of victory against the enemy, tremendous emphasis was placed on the necessity of the Indian child's acquiring at least a "speaking acquaintance" with the English language. Students were forbidden to speak their native tongue at all in some classrooms. It is said that Puerto Ricans or Poles find it easier to learn the English language, after immigrating to New York or Detroit than for the Navajos to learn it (at that time), living in remote areas where they rarely heard it spoken.

Not only was general education at a very low ebb, the economy of the tribe was also suffering. In addition to the devastation of their land, culminating in the infamous "Long Walk" of 1864, the Navajos had suffered the insult of seizure of vast areas of land by ruthless white stockmen. The people had reason to resent the white man, but in spite of all, when the country was endangered, they rallied to the colors.

According to an article in *The Leatherneck* (March, 1948), on December 7, E. M. Fryer, Indian Reservation superintendent, looked out of his window to see a large number of Navajo youths who had gathered in a clearing, their faces grim. Some carried personal effects in big red bandanas, knotted at the corners. All were armed and carried ammunition. When Mr. Fryer inquired as to the cause of the gathering, they answered: "We're going to fight."[1]

Hours later, the youths were prevailed upon to return to their hogans and await the official call to arms that inevitably would come.

It is said that one tribe in New Mexico saw all of its fighting men clean and oil their rifles, pack their saddlebags and ride to Gallup, prepared to enter battle then and there.

After the official call to arms was issued, the Navajos appeared at their agencies, carrying old muskets and hunting rifles, asking where they could fight the enemy. Many were turned away, heartbroken and humiliated that they could not fight because they could not speak English. One writer said, "Although the 'Great White Father' has often regarded the Indians as step-children, these First Americans sprang to the front line of defense when the chips were down."

Navajos were destined to fight in every theatre of that far-flung war—from the Aleutian Islands to North Africa, on the Normandy beaches, in Sicily and Italy, and—most of all—in the Central and South Pacific.

The Navajos had no idea when the war broke out that they would ultimately play a significant part in the prosecution of that war—particularly against Japan. They could not know that they were to be selected to carry out a special mission that no other group could perform. Even when recruiters visited the boarding schools, culling out the young men with good minds and strong bodies—fit for a rugged, demanding life in the Marines—the Navajos did not know that they were indeed

1. Vernon Langille, "Indian War Call," *The Leatherneck,* vol. 31-A, March, 1948, p. 37.

"the chosen people." These young men were selected to become combat communications specialists—the first of a kind.

The commanders in the Pacific were aware of stolen codes and new codes the enemy could easily decipher. One writer said, "Military communications were being made available to the enemy like sand sifting through a sieve."

On Guadalcanal, the First Marine Division was slowly grinding its way toward victory; but almost from the firing of the first gun on the island, the need for a new swift code became painfully obvious. One correspondent reported, "When the fighting became confined to a small area, everything had to move on a split-second schedule. There was not time for enciphering and deciphering which ordinary code requires. At such times, the King's English became a last resort—the profaner the better."

But this method could hardly be called effective, for many of the Japanese could speak English fluently, and were acquainted with terms of American profanity. At one time, when a battalion CO asked his company commander for the exact position of a reconnaissance patrol along the Lunga River, the answer came in "grid coordinates." A third voice cut in on the two-way communication: "Thank you. Our patrol will be there too." The cunning Japanese demonstrated time and again their great facility for wiretapping, and their infuriating understanding of our language.

Eventually a complex code system was devised for general use, but the immediate need for quick and accurate message transmission was to be filled by the Navajo code talkers! Their code was to be a secret weapon!

Chapter Two

THE PILOT PROJECT

... These are excellent translations!

An aura of mystery has always enveloped the idea of cryptography. In the early years, codes (systems of secret message transmission) were associated somewhat with the occult —perhaps because astrologists used mysterious symbols for the planets. Perhaps the most famous of the early references to this kind of message (the use of words with hidden meanings) is that of the Biblical "handwriting on the wall," which Daniel interpreted for the king Belshazzar.

During World War II, Rear Admiral S. Anderson, once director of Naval Intelligence, referred to the fantastic methods developed by American cryptographers to decipher Japanese codes as MAGIC. The term stuck!

Tokyo was at the time using devious methods of conveying messages (with hidden meanings) in what appeared to be innocent weather forecasts (by radio). They referred to countries in these forecasts as follows: "east wind rain" for the United States; "north wind cloudy" for Russia and "west wind clear" for England. (These weather terms might remind one of the "code" used by the astronauts in Apollo 13 when they asked the center at Houston if the flowers were blooming there. The meaning of the question was revealed later. They were inquiring if the man who was left behind had yet contracted measles.)

During World War II, coded names were applied to secret projects. For instance, the Anglo-American invasion of North Africa was known as "Operation Touch," the attack on

Salerno as "Avalanche," and the Allies' attack on the Marshall Islands as "Flintlock." Plans for the operation to take Guadalcanal and Tulagi were called "Watchtower"; however, those who thought the forces too meager to accomplish the task dubbed the plan "Operation Shoestring."

The method of using regional or ancient languages not used in everyday life has been tried with varying degrees of success. It is said that the Allies facetiously transmitted some fake messages in Yiddish on the Italian front during World War II; any German who admitted that he was familiar with the language was in danger of being shipped out to a concentration camp.

Back in World War I, eight Choctaws in Company D, 141st Infantry were instructed to transmit orders by field telephone, an operation that proved successful. The Germans were adept at deciphering our codes during World War II, a fact that prodded an officer to use two Comanche Indians as a team for transmitting and receiving messages by telephone. It appeared thereafter that not a syllable of the messages was intelligible to the enemy. The Comanches were used frequently in a similar capacity in subsequent action.

Actually, during World War II, Indians of many tribes spoke across enemy lines in Africa, Sicily and the South Pacific—Comanche, Creek, Choctaw, Menominee, Chippewa, and Hopi. But in each case the Indians were speaking in their own tongue—not in code.

Credit for the concept of the use of a code based on the Navajo language and the presentation of the idea to the Marines goes to a man named Philip Johnston, an engineer for the city of Los Angeles at the outbreak of the war. Mr. Johnston had spent the major part of his life on the reservation and spoke the language fluently.

His life with the Navajos began when, at the age of four, his Protestant missionary father, William Riley Johnston, and his mother, Margaret, took him to the reservation. During those early childhood years, he had only Indian children to play with, and being with them long hours of the day, he naturally learned to speak their language, and in addition learned their songs, their ceremonies, and much of their tradition.

As he grew a little older, he served as a translator for his father, other missionaries, and government agents on the reservation. At the age of nine he accompanied his father and two Navajos to the White House where Mr. Johnston appealed to President Theodore Roosevelt for fair treatment of the Navajos and Hopis. Little Philip served as interpreter. He remembers to this day the fact that President Roosevelt ruffled his hair and greeted him with, "Hello, Philip!"

He entered the service at the time of World War I and served in the 319th Engineers in France for a year. He returned home in 1919, entered the University of Southern California in 1921, graduating with a degree in civil engineering. From this time on, he worked for the Bureau of Engineering in the city of Los Angeles, lecturing on his life with the Navajos on the side.

With this rich background, it is not surprising that the Navajos came to mind as a possible "secret weapon" against the enemy when war broke out against Japan. It all started when he saw a newspaper story one day concerning an armored division on practice maneuvers in Louisiana where they were trying out a unique idea for secret communication—attempting to establish some sort of system using several of their Indian personnel. The news item sparked the concept of a *code* based on the complex Navajo tongue.

The following day he confronted Lieutenant Colonel James E. Jones, Area Signal Officer at Camp Elliott, seven miles north of San Diego, and asked, "Colonel, what would you think of a device that would assure you of complete secrecy when you send or receive messages on the battlefield?" The officer responded, "In all the history of warfare, that has never been done. No code, no cipher is completely secure from enemy interception. We change our codes frequently for this reason."

Mr. Johnston pursued the presentation of his idea, suggesting that the kind of code he had in mind would be based on an Indian language, would always be used orally by radio or telephone, and would never be reduced to writing that might fall into enemy hands.

The colonel reminded Mr. Johnston that such a plan had been tried during World War I by Canadian forces against the Germans; however, it had not worked because the Indians had no words in their vocabulary that were equivalents for military terms. He felt sure the idea would not be practical.

Mr. Johnston continued, "My plan is *not* to use translations of an Indian language, but to build up a *code* of Indian words." He said, "Let's imagine this code included terms such as 'fast shooter' to designate a machine gun, and 'iron rain' for a barrage. Navajo personnel would be thoroughly drilled to understand and use these substitutions."

To prove how bewildering the Navajo language can be to a non-Navajo, Mr. Johnston uttered a few phrases in the language he knew so well. The performance was persuasive enough for Colonel Jones to say, "O.K., Mr. Johnston! You may have something there. I'd like very much to see some of these Navajos!" It was decided that a demonstration on this proposed code would be made before Marine officers who would evaluate the idea.

The Navajo tongue is an extremely difficult language to master, and should a non-Navajo (particularly German or Japanese) learn to speak it, counterfeiting its sounds would be almost impossible. A language ideal as a basis for a cryptosystem of extremely high, if not impregnable security! The words must be produced with a precision that is difficult for any adult to master, particularly because of the complexity of the verb forms of the language. The verb stem depends on the object acted upon—whether it be a fabric, a solid object, a round mass or what-have-you.

Having grown up with the Navajos, Philip Johnston had complete faith in their ability to "come through" on this difficult assignment—that of providing security on tactical radio nets and related systems—since it had been proved in the Pacific that using secure codes of a cryptographic nature was at times cumbersome.

Two weeks after he presented his case for the formation and utilization of a Navajo code, he returned to the office of Lieutenant-Colonel Jones, at Camp Elliott, and announced that he had found educated tribesmen in Los Angeles through an employment agency conducted solely for Indians. He could now proceed with a demonstration as to how the code could be used.

"We're all ready for you," was the response. "A field telephone has been installed in Headquarters Building. Here are six typical messages used in operations. See what the men can do with them."

At the appointed time, Philip Johnston brought the men he had located to the colonel's office and they were taken to the headquarters of Major General Clayton B. Vogel. The room was full of "high brass," including Colonel Wethered Woodward, who had been sent out from the Marine Corps Division of Plans and Policies. Two of the Navajos were taken to another room and the test began.

The military messages given to the men in English were transmitted in Navajo, and then retranslated into English. Fifteen minutes later, the general inspected the results. Amazed and delighted, he exclaimed, "These are excellent translations! As good as might be possible from any language. There's no doubt in my mind that Navajo words could be used for code purposes. I shall request the Commandant to authorize such a project immediately."

In February (1942), Mr. Johnston, a meticulously thorough man, prepared a document which Major General Vogel forwarded to the Commandant of the United States Marine Corps in March, along with a letter asking for the recruitment of Navajo Indians to be used as communicators.

In his document, he presented a brief history of American

Indians, a discussion of their various languages, and pointed out the particular complexity of the Navajo tongue. He wrote, "This tribe is selected as an example of a possible plan for recruitment because of the writer's intimate knowledge of its reservation, the people and their language."

He outlined in detail his plan for the Navajos to render this unique service to the United States, and suggested locations for the special recruiting service. (See Appendix, Item I.)

A month later, Commanding General Clayton B. Vogel of Camp Elliott sent a letter to the Commandant of the United States Marine Corps praising the demonstration given by the Navajos in San Diego, and recommending that an effort be made to enlist 200 Navajo Indians for this communications force. He wrote: "In addition to linguistic qualifications in English and their tribal dialect they should have the physical qualifications necessary for messengers." (See Appendix, Item II.)

Even in wartime, Washington often seems maddeningly slow to anyone who is desperately trying to get a program started. Major General Vogel's enthusiasm was met with skepticism and his request for two hundred recruits was countered with permission to recruit an initial group of 30 as a "pilot project."

In April, four months after the holocaust at Pearl Harbor, Marine Corps recruiters went to the Navajo reservation to select the first group of code talkers. They signed up the authorized number from boarding schools at Fort Defiance, Fort Wingate and Shiprock. For some reason, one man either withdrew or was withdrawn from the group, leaving 29 in the initial project.

Recently Ted Evans, director of Veterans Affairs for the Navajo Nation said,

I've always heard that there were supposed to be 30 Navajos in that first unit, and only 29 showed up. I think *I* am that 30th man! Some of the boys in that first group were in my class at high school, and I was interviewed along with them (this was in 1942). But I wanted to play foot-ball, so they gave me leave until after the foot-ball season. During the last two games, I got hurt in the knee. That put me out so I had to work as a civilian until 1944 when I was accepted by the army.

Organized as the 382nd Platoon, U.S. Marine Corps, the 29 men included the following: Frank Pete, Willsie Bitsie, Chester Nez, Eugene Crawford, John Brown, Cosey Brown, John Benally, William Yazzie (now known as Dean Wilson), Benjamin Cleveland, Nelson Thompson, Lloyd Oliver, Charlie Begay, William McCabe, Oscar Ilthma, David Curley, Lowell Damon, Balmer Slowtalker, Alfred Leonard, Dale June, James Dixon, Roy Begay, James Manuelito, Harry Tsosie, George Dennison, Carl Gorman, Samuel Begay, John Chee, Jack Nez and John Willie.

The twenty-nine original Navajo code talkers and three officers.

Chapter Three

THE NAVAJOS AS MARINES

... The same gripes.

To most of the Navajos in those early days, getting on a train, plane or bus to go to who-knew-where was as forbidding as our going to the moon. One observer commented that the Navajos who signed up with the Marines were Neil Armstrongs in their way—going to the great unknown. He added that most of us would think that basic training, learning better English, getting accustomed to eating with knife and fork would be nothing—the fighting and shooting would be the hard part. But the latter was the easiest part of all for the Navajos. The most difficult element in the whole thing was leaving the reservation and *getting* there—going to a strange part of the world. However, the orientation period for the Navajos at camp was not as difficult as the officers in charge feared it might be.

One of the Indians reported, "When we got to camp at San Diego, they said, 'Clear out your pockets.' So we did—hunting knives, gum, chewing tobacco, etc. I had a stockman's knife with a six-inch blade; I never saw it again, and I had carried it for about ten years!"

In talking about this first experience off the reservation, another code talker recalls that, after they had turned over all personal gear, they were issued fresh supplies of whatever was standard at that time—safety razor, shaving soap, etc. Most of the men in the group had never shaved in their lives. They were too young! Some were only fifteen years old. He says, "One of our men had one or two whiskers and the sergeant

14

came up to him for close inspection and yelled, 'Did you shave this morning?' 'No, sir!' was the answer. 'I've never shaved in my life!' The sergeant then asked, 'Did we issue you a razor? Then go in and use it!'

One code talker recently commented, "When we were recruited, we knew only that we were to be specialists of some kind, but did not know we would have anything to do with the setting up of the code. When we got to camp we thought we were in a penitentiary, after the free life on the reservation. We had to wear a shabby arrangement of dungarees. Training was grueling out in that hot sun in San Diego."

One of the Navajos describes the way they felt during those somewhat traumatic first days in strange surroundings, living in an entirely new life style:

We had never been under any discipline before we entered boot camp. We had lived out in the sheep country. So this was shocking to us. The sergeant didn't make things any easier for us. That first night he came storming in and said, "You guys were civilians, weren't you?" "Yes, sir!" "Well, you're not civilians any more! Stand up to attention! You're Marines now!" So we all stood up and he commenced to show us how to fix our bed—a couple sheets, blanket, etc.

When we went to bed that night, one of the guys was sniffling, and when I woke up in the middle of the night, he was moaning and crying, and said he didn't know how in the world he had ever gotten into this. Now we were all volunteers, but here he was groaning and talking to himself, and wondering why he had gotten into the Marine Corps.

The next morning, we fixed our beds exactly as the sergeant had showed us—to the very crease. When he came in, he stood at the foot of the beds and threw the covers all over on the floor and yelled, "Fix them the way I showed you!" That day each of us did the bunks about five times.

This code talker admits that many humorous things happened along with the hardships. He relates these incidents:

15

We were in columns of three on the parade ground one day when we were given orders to "rear march." The first six guys in front didn't hear the command. They just kept walking. So the officer called a halt and we halted. He called "Halt!" to the first six men, but they didn't hear him and kept walking. The sergeant sprinted up to the head of the line and called, "About face!" When the six turned around, the rest of us were 'way back. The sergeant mumbled, "Those six deaf Indians can't hear the commands. I don't know what they're here for! I think they ought to be sent back to the reservation!"

One of our sergeants was mighty quick with his fists. He didn't like the way we were boxing one day. You see we aren't aggressive in nature; we were always peaceful, but he made us box. We pretended we were hitting real hard, but he yelled, "That's no way to box!" So he lined us up, and came down the line boxing each of us . . . wham . . . wham . . . wham. We were falling all over the place. It seems that one of our guys had had some training in boxing, and when the sergeant got to him, and reared back to deliver that mean punch, this Navajo gave it to him. Well . . . that was the last of our boxing matches.

Colonel James H. Tinsley (a white Marine who was with the 21st Regiment of the Third Division on Bougainville) recalls boxing matches in which Navajo was set against Navajo. He says, "It was hilarious—long on energy, but completely lacking in skill." Their hearts weren't in it!

Another Navajo describes a humorous incident that occurred in training one day:

We were told we were an honor platoon—the best! Another platoon competing with us was counting cadence in Chinese (they had a few Chinese in their ranks). Our sergeant got the idea that we ought to count cadence in Navajo. Well, we'd go three or four steps while we were counting "one." He didn't know what we were saying, so right there we mixed things up, using some bad words. Then

16

we got to laughing so hard we couldn't march. We were all doubled up right there on the parade ground. The sergeant got mad and lined us up again. We started out naming everybody and everything, counting cadence, calling him names as we went along. Finally we just couldn't go anymore, so he said, "O.K.! I've caught on. No more counting in Navajo!"

Louis D. Steinbacher, who served in the Radio Platoon in the Fourth Signal Company laughingly recalls the way in which a Navajo buddy named George Yoe always answered roll call. A Marine was expected to answer with his own name, followed by "Here," "Yoh," or "Present." For example, "Jones here, sir!" Private Yoe invariably responded with "Yoe, yoh, sir!" (This particular battalion was standing inspection once, when the colonel decided to check a Navajo's canteen to see if there was water in it. He was sorry he did—he was sprayed with warm beer.)

One of the code-talker recruits relates one of his experiences at boot camp that completely changed his whole life in service. At one time during training, he felt he could not stand the stress any longer and finally "went over the hill." He started back to the reservation and had been absent from camp three days when he decided he had made a grave mistake. He turned back to "face the music." Not far from camp, a busload of WAVEs stopped and picked him up. When they asked him when he had to be back in camp, he told them there was really no hurry. So he spent his last day of freedom with a busload of good-looking girls. The bus rolled up to the gate and was given the O.K. sign to enter. The Navajo flashed his identification and with no questions asked, he rolled right into camp with the WAVEs.

Eventually, of course, he was brought up before the officers who demanded to know where he had been, how he had gotten back into camp, etc. He admitted that he had gone AWOL and told the truth as to how he got back in. They wouldn't believe him and asked him to come up with a better story than this—this one they couldn't believe. After insisting that he had told them God's truth, he realized that they would never believe him. So he fabricated the story that he had watched the guards and when they weren't looking, he had sneaked in under the fence. *This* the officers believed.

As for punishment—rather than locking him up, making him serve time and what-have-you, they promised to release him without punishment if he would agree to transfer to the Reconnaissance Company of the Fifth Division. Since this was the only way out, he agreed, not knowing that the men in this area of service were assigned to the most hazardous operations in the combat areas. (It should be noted here that his heart was with the code talkers, and in the Pacific he spent as much time with them as he could, catching up on what they had learned after he had deserted camp.)

In some instances, non-Navajos, instructing the recruits in general Marine Corps activities, found it difficult to "get through" the Indian's baffling imperturbability. But the Navajos took to rigid discipline well, marched with precision and kept their quarters unusually clean. One day after inspection, the major sent a special message to one platoon early in the communications program: "The Commanding Officer commends the Navajo School for the neatness of their quarters." Their officer responded, "The Navajos try harder!"

The Navajos' spartan way of life, which included bathing in the snow, had hardened them so much that even members of other tribes called them "the toughest men on earth."

The white Marines marveled at the skills of the Indians and accepted them readily. Race friction was unknown. The men worked and played together, after the Indians had overcome a certain understandable initial shyness. In a tug of war between equal numbers of white and Indian Marines, the Navajos usually won.

One code talker insists that there is little difference in the physical prowess of the Anglos and Navajos. However, he admits that when the general inspected dress parade on one very hot day, some of the white Marines fainted but the Navajos remained ramrod straight and upright.

The Navajos tend to be a little shorter than their white brothers. One is remembered as having the smallest feet in the entire Marine Corps. He wore size-four shoes, and had to pack Kleenex in the toes of his boots.

One man recalls the day in boot camp when the Navajo platoon was doing so well they were sure they would get the nomination for first place on Saturday's inspection. All of them were short with the exception of one—a rather tall man. They were the last to pass in review and that tall guy was out of step, so the platoon came out second!

Another Navajo remembers the way the sergeant of the all-Indian platoon would yell, "All right, you stump-jumpers! Get going!"

A writer for the *Marine Corps Chevron* reported that the Navajos had taken to Marine life and general training like ducks to water. He wrote, "At present, they're a typical Marine outfit of budding specialists. They gripe about the things that all Marines gripe about—liberty, chow, and the San Diego weather."[2] It appears that the men asked for little, and seemed generally adaptable to all situations in this new and different environment.

The *Headquarters Bulletin* (another Marine publication) carried a story in which it was reported that "some came dressed like their white brothers but many came wearing items of native dress such as headbands and moccasins. They knew little of the assembly line procedure of issuing clothing and medical examination, but quickly learned whys and wherefores of military life."

The reporter praised the men for their quick mastery of the intricacies of modern weapons. "They learned to climb mock-ups instead of pueblo ladders," he wrote, and "instructors couldn't think of any strenuous drill on forced marches too

2. "Navajos Readying to Going Tough for Japanazis," *Marine Corps Chevron,* January 23, 1943, p. 1.

tough for the braves. When the day was done, the Indians laughed at the drudgery of the hard routine."[3]

On May 7, 1943 (some time later in the program), G. R. Lockard, commanding officer of the Special and Service Battalion of the First Amphibious Corps at Camp Goettge, sent the following communication to the commanding general of the same corps:

> As general duty Marines, the Navajos are without peers. As individuals and as a group, these people are scrupulously clean, neat and orderly. They quickly learn to adapt themselves to the conditions of the service. They are quiet and uncomplaining; in eight months I have received only one complaint—a just one. In short, Navajos make good Marines, and I should be very proud to command a unit composed entirely of these people.

Early in the program, the men at Camp Elliott decided to stage a ceremonial dance for the camp. It proved to be an elaborate affair, including dancing, talking about the code, and singing. The Navajos are said to be ready to sing "at the drop of a hat," which is a surprise for those who do not know them. And they sing well! The song they performed for the program at Camp Elliott had never been presented anywhere in the world before . . . the tune, but not the words.

Jimmy King, a Navajo instructor in the school, translated the Marine Hymn into the Navajo language. As reported in *Marine Corps Chevron*, January 23, 1943, "It's really something to hear forty-odd Navajos swing out on the cocky-sounding 'Hymn' in Navajo-ese."

Mr. King's English version of the Marine Hymn follows:

> We have conquered our enemies
> All over the world.
> On land and on sea,
> Everywhere we fight.

3. "Red Man Hits the War Path," *Headquarters Bulletin*, September, 1944, p. 19.

True and loyal to our duty.
  We are known by that.
United States Marines,
  To be one is a great thing.

Our flag waves
  From dawn to setting sun.
We have fought every place
  Where we could take a gun.
From northern lands
  To southern tropic scenes,
We are known to be tireless,
  The United States Marines.

(Last verse like a prayer)

May we live in peace hereafter.
  We have conquered all our foes.
No force in the world we cannot conquer,
  We know of no fear.
If the Army and the Navy
  Ever look on Heaven's scenes,
United States Marines will be there
  Living in peace.

Here is the Hymn in Navajo-ese:

Nin hokeh bi-kheh a-na-ih-la
  Ta-al-tso-go na-he-seel-kai
Nih-bi-kah-gi do tah kah-gi
  Ta-al-tso-go en-da-de-pah
Tsi-di-da-an-ne ne-tay-yah
  Ay be nihe hozeen
Washindon be Akalh Bi-kosi-la
  Ji-lengo ba-hozhon

Ni-he da-na-ah-taj ihla
  Yel khol-go e-e-ah

Day-ne tal-al-tso go enta-she-jah
  Tal-tso-go en-tas-se-pah
Ha-kaz dineh-ih be-hay-yah
  Ado ta a-khek-ash-shen
Do ni-din-da-hi ol-yeh
  Washindon be Akalh-bi-Khos.

Hozo-go nay-yel-tay to
  A-na-oh bi-keh de-dlihn
Ni-hi-keh di-dlini ta-etin
  Yeh-wol-ye hi-he a-din
Sila-go-tsoi do chah-lakai
  Ya-ansh-go das dez-ee
Washindon be Akalh-bi-kosi la
  Hozo-go kay-ha-tihn.

Chapter Four

THE NAVAJO CODE

...A is for Ant—also for Wol-la-chee.

The initial group of twenty-nine Navajos combined rigorous physical training with methods in communications (such as Morse code and semaphores); in addition, they attacked the formidable task of constructing the code—the job for which they had been particularly selected. It was eventually to include 211 words most frequently used in the military lexicon, supplemented by an alphabet to spell out proper names and other words not included in the syllabus.

One code talker (who had lied about his age and was only sixteen at the time) has commented that they "wrung their minds dry" trying to figure out words that would be usable, that would not be too long, and that could be easily memorized. After all, in the heat of battle, the code talker would have no time to take out a chart and look up vocabulary for an urgent message. The men tried to choose words that had a direct association with that which was familiar in their life on the reservation, or within their general knowledge.

All the recruits spoke basically the same Navajo, but there were certain word variations. In Navajo the same word spoken with four different inflections will carry four different meanings. The group had to agree on words that have no fine shades of interpretation, for any variation in an urgent military message might be disastrous in the loss of advantage, and in loss of life.

Many words were taken directly from nature. For instance,

the equivalent for observation plane was *owl*, for bomber, *buzzard*, for fighter plane, *hummingbird*, for dive bomber, *chicken hawk*, for January, *crusted snow*, for July, *small harvest*, for August, *big harvest*, for March, *squeaky voice*, for amphibious, *frog*, for battleship, *whale*, for cruiser, *small whale*, for destroyer, *beaver*, for route, *rabbit trail*, etc.

Words for letters of the alphabet were mostly names of animals; for example, *ant* for A, *mouse* for M, *pig* for P, *turkey* for T, and *weasel* for W.

Following is the complete initial code, devised by the original group of twenty-nine Navajo recruits:

Alphabet

A	(Wol-la-chee)	Ant
B	(Shush)	Bear
C	(Moasi)	Cat
D	(Be)	Deer
E	(Dzeh)	Elk
F	(Ma-e)	Fox
G	(Klizzie)	Goat
H	(Lin)	Horse
I	(Tkin)	Ice
J	(Tkele-cho-gi)	Jackass
K	(Klizzie-yazzie)	Kid
L	(Dibeh-yazzie)	Lamb
M	(Na-as-tso-si)	Mouse
N	(Nesh-chee)	Nut
O	(Ne-ahs-jsh)	Owl
P	(Bi-sodih)	Pig
Q	(Ca-yeilth)	Quiver
R	(Gah)	Rabbit
S	(Dibeh)	Sheep
T	(Than-zie)	Turkey
U	(No-da-ih)	Ute
V	(A-keh-di-glini)	Victor
W	(Gloe-ih)	Weasel
X	(Al-an-as-dzoh)	Cross
Y	(Tsah-as-zih)	Yucca
Z	(Besh-do-gliz)	Zinc

Names of various organizations:

Corps	Din-neh-ih	Clan
Division	Ashi-hi	Salt

Regiment	Tabaha	Edge Water
Battalion	Tacheene	Red Soil
Company	Nakia	Mexican
Platoon	Has-clish-nih	Mud
Section	Yo-ih	Beads
Squad	Debeh-li-zini	Black Sheet

Terms for communications:

Telephone	Besh-hal-ne-ih	Telephone
Switchboard	Ya-ih-e-tih-ih	Central
Wire	Besh-le-chee-ih	Copper
Telegraph	Besh-le-chee-ih-beh-hane-ih	Communication by copper wire
Semaphore	Dah-ha-a-tah-ih-beh-hane-ih	Flag signals
Blinker	Coh-nil-kol-lih	Fire blinder
Radio	Nil-chi-hal-ne-ih	Radio
Panels	Az-kad-be-ha-ne-ih	Carpet signals

Terms for officers (A-la-jih-na-zini)—Headmen:

Major General	So-na-kih	Two Stars
Brigadier General	So-a-la-ih	One Star
Colonel	Atsah-besh-le-gai	Silver Eagle
Lieutenant Colonel	Che-chil-be-tah-besh-legai	Silver Oak Leaf
Major	Che-chil-be-tah-ola	Gold Oak Leaf
Captain	Besh-legai-na-kih	Two Silver Bars
First Lieutenant	Besh-legai-a-lah-ih	One Silver Bar
Second Lieutenant	Ola-alah-ih-ni-ahi	One Gold Bar

Terms for airplanes (Wo-tah-de-ne-ih)—Air Force:

Dive bomber	Gini	Chicken hawk
Torpedo plane	Tas-chizzie	Swallow
Observation plane	Ne-as-jah	Owl
Fighter plane	Da-he-tih-hi	Hummingbird
Bomber	Jay-sho	Buzzard
Patrol plane	Ga-gih	Crow
Transport	Atsah	Eagle

Terms for ships (Toh-dineh-ih)—Sea Force:

Battleship	Lo-tso	Whale
Aircraft carrier	Tsidi-ney-ye-hi	Bird carrier
Submarine	Besh-lo	Iron fish
Mine sweeper	Cha	Beaver
Destroyer	Ca-lo	Shark

Transport	Dineh-nay-ye-hi	Man carrier
Cruiser	Lo-tso-yazzie	Small whale
Mosquito boat	Tse-e	Mosquito

Names of months:

January	Yas-nil-tes	Crusted snow
February	Atsah-be-yaz	Small eagle
March	Woz-cheind	Squeaky voice
April	Tsah-chill	Small plant
May	Tah-tso	Big plant
June	Be-he-eh-eh-jah-tso	Big planting
July	Be-he-ta-tsosie	Small harvest
August	Be-heen-ta-tso	Big harvest
September	Ghan-jih	Half
October	Nil-chi-tsosie	Small wind
November	Nil-chi-tso	Big wind
December	Kesh-mesh	Christmas

General vocabulary:

Action	Ah-ha-tinh	Place of action
Advance	Nas-say	Ahead
Airdrome	Nilchi-began	Air house
Alert	Ha-ih-des-ee	Watchful
Allies	Nih-hi-cho	Our friends
Along	Wolachee-snez	Long ant
Also	Eh-do	Also
Alternate	Na-kee-go-ne-nan-dey-he	Second position
Amphibious	Chal	Frog
And	Do	Also
Annex	Ih-nay-tani	Addition
Approach	Bi-chi-ol-dah	Moving to
Are	Gah-tso	Large rabbit
Area	Haz-a-gih	Area
Armored	Besh-ye-ha-da-di-teh	Iron protected
Arrive	Il-day	Came
Army	Lei-cha-ih-yil-knee-ih	Dog faces
Artillery	Be-al-doh-tso-lani	Many big guns
As	Ahce	Ace
Assault	Altseh-e-jah-he	First striker
Attached	A-hid-day-tih	Attached
Available	Ta-shoz-teh-ih	Available
Battery	Bih-be-al-doh-tka-ih	Three guns
Base	Bih-tsee-dih	Foundation
Be	Tses-nah	Bee

26

Been	Tses-nah-nes-chee	Bee nut
Before	Bih-tse-dih	Prior
Begin	Ha-hol-ziz	Commenced from
Belong	Tses-nah-snez	Long bee
Block	Da-dey-thah	Block
Bombs	A-ye-shi	Eggs
By	Be-gha	By
Camp	To-altseh-hogan	Temporary place
Camouflage	Di-nes-ih	Hid
Can	Yah-di-zini	Can
Cannoneer	Be-al-doh-tso-dey-dey-dil-don-igi	Big gun operator
Capacity	Be-nel-ah	Capacity
Capitol	Tkah-chae	Sweat house
Captured	Yis-nah	Captured
Casualty	Bih-din-ne-dey	Put out of action
Class	Alth-ah-a-teh	Class
Coast Guard	Ta-bas-dsissi	Shore runner
Code	Yil-tas	Peck
Column	Alth-kay-ni-zih	Column
Combat	Da-ah-hi-jih-ganh	Fighting
Combination	Al-tkas-ei	Mixed
Commander	Bih-keh-he	Senior
Commanding officer	Hash-kay-gi-na-tah	War Chief
Concentrate	Ta-la-hi-jih	One place
Confidential	Na-nil-in	Kept secret
Conquered	A-keh-des-dlin	Won
Convoy	Tkal-kah-o-nel	Moving on water
Counter-attack	Woltah-al-ki-gi-jeh	Counteract
Creek	Toh-nil-tsanh	Very little water
Debouchment	Dzilth-ganh-ih	Apache
Defense	Ah-kin-gil-toh	Defense
Department	Hogan	Department
Dispositions	A-ho-tay	Dispositions
Displace	Hih-do-nal	Move
Do	Tse-le	Small pup
Echelon	Who-dzoh	Line
Engineer	Day-dil-jah-hi	Fire builder
Enlist	Bih-zih-a-da-yi-lah	Written signature
Escape	A-zeh-ha-ge-yah	Escape
Establish	Has-tay-dzah	Setup
Estimate	Bih-ke-tse-shod-des-kez	Estimate
Execute	A-do-nil	Will happen
Fail	Cha-al-cind	Fail
Field	Clo-dih	Outside
Fire	Coh	Fire

Flank	Dah-di-kad	Flank
Flare	Wo-chi	Light streak
Grenades	Ni-ma-si	Potatoes
Guard	Ni-dih-da-hi	Guard
Have	Jo	Have
H.E.	Be-al-doh-be-ca-bih-dzil-igi	Powerful shell
Headquarters	Na-ha-tah-ba-hogan	Headquarters
Hospital	A-zey-al-ih	Place of medicine
Install	Ehd-thah	Install
Invade	A-tah-gi-nah	Moved into
Is	Seis	Seven
Island	Seis-keyah	Seven land
Left	Nish-cla-jih-na-nee-goh	Left side
Location	A-kew-eh	Spot
Machine gun	A-knah-as-donih	Rapid-fire gun
Magnetic	Na-e-lahi	Pick up
Maneuver	Na-na-o-nalth	Moving around
Manufacture	Besh-be-eh-el-ih-dih	Metal factory
Mechanic	Chiti-a-nayl-inih	Auto repairman
Message	Hane-al-neh	Message
Military	Silago-keh-goh	Military
Mine	Ha-gade	Mine
Mortar	Be-al-doh-cid-da-hi	Sitting gun
Navy	Tal-kah-Silago	Sea soldiers
No	Beh-bih-ke-as-chinigig	What's written
Not	Ni-dah-tkanzio	No turkey
Objective	Bi-ne-yei	Goal
Observed	Hal-zid	Observed
Occurred	Yeel-tsod	Taken
Of	Toh-ni-tkal-lo	Ocean fish
Or	Eh-dodah-goh	Either
Order	Be-eh-ho-zini	Direction
Ordnance	Lei-az-jah	Underground
Overlay	Be-ka-has-tsoz	Overlay
Parenthesis	Atsanh	Rib
Penalize	Tah-ni-des-tanh	Set back
Primary	Altseh-nan-day-hi-gih	First position
Proceed	Nay-nih-jih	Go
Protect	Ah-chanh	Self-defense
Railhead	A-do-geh-hi	Shipping and receiving point
Rallying	A-lah-na-o-glalth	Gathering
Range	An-zeh	Distance
Reached	Baz-ni-tsood	Reached

Receipt	Shoz-teh	Receipt
Reconnaissance	Ha-a-cidi	Inspector
Reinforce	Nal-dzil	Reinforce
Relieved	Nah-jih-co-nal-ya	Removed
Replacement	Ni-na-do-nil	Replacement
Report	Who-neh	Got words
Representative	Tka-naz-nili	Triple men
Request	Jo-kayed-goh	Ask for
Retreat	Ji-din-ned-chanh	Surrender
River	Toh-yil-kal	Much water
Route	Gah-bih-tkeen	Rabbit trail
Runner	Nih-dzid-teih	Runner
Sabotage	A-tkel-yah	Hindered
Saboteur	A-tkel-el-ini	Troublemaker
Sailors	Cha-le-gai	White caps
Seaman	Tkal-kah-dineh-ih	Seaman
Secret	Bah-has-tkin	Secret
Side	Bosh-keesh	Side
Signal	Na-eh-eh-gish	By sign
Shell	Be-al-doh-be-ca	Shell
Short	Be-oh	Short
Space	Be-tkah	Between
Stream	Toh-ni-lin	Running water
Submerged	Tkal-cla-yi-yah	Went under water
Submit	A-nih-leh	Send
Such	Yis-cleh	Sox
Supplementary	Tka-go-ne-nan-dey-he	Third position
Supply	Nal-yeh-hi	Supply
Territory	Ke-yah	Land
That	Tkanzie-cha	Turkey hat
The	Cha-gee	Blue jay
Their	Bih	Their
They	Ni-ghai	They
Together	Ta-bil	With
Torpedo	Lobe-ca	Fish shell
Tracer	Beh-na-al-kah-hi	Tracer
Traffic diagram	Hane-ba-na-as-dzoh	Diagram-story line
Troops	Nal-deh-hi	Troops
Unit	Da-az-jah	Bunched
Vicinity	Na-hos-ah-gih	There about
Was	Ne-teh	Was
Weapons	Beh-dah-a-hi-jah-geni	Fighting weapons
Wire	Besh-tsosie	Thin wire
Zone	Bah-na-has-dzoh	Area

The next step in mastering the use of the code was a matter

of dictation. Navajo words in the vocabulary were spoken by the instructor, and each member of the class was asked to print the English equivalent on a test sheet. For instance:

Navajo term read	*English equivalent*
Let's go	Forward
Short big gun	Howitzer
In place	Installation
Know other's action	Liaison
Cliff dwelling	Fortification

The next phase of training had to do with using code words in giving operational orders. A manual compiled by the Marine Corps, entitled "Sample Operations Orders," was used as a basis for this. Orders were read *in the code* by the instructor, and the members of the class printed English translations on their test sheets. Following are examples taken from the manual:

Reached objective at 1945, am reorganizing.
Enemy riflemen under the protection of heavy artillery support.
Machine-gun fire on right flank.
Continue to advance.
Consolidate your position.
Landing wave on beach, but losses high.
Am forced to dig in.

The last two weeks of the eight-week course were devoted to experience in the field, and learning the operation and care of all signal equipment.

In simulated battles, Navajo messages were sent over the air from moving positions—planes to ground, ship to shore, and from tanks and half-tracks to the message center. Navajos not in the code program were sent into the field to attempt to decipher the messages, but they failed.

Messages transmitted included information about the enemy (known or estimated strength, composition and disposition of their forces) and instructions for Allied forces having to do with attachments, scheme of maneuver, mission or objective, direction of attack, general locations or direction of principal efforts, assistance to be rendered to other units, routes of advance, assembly disposition or time of attack.

One code talker facetiously says, "We also had to be able to tell the general where it would be safe for him to take his coffee break."

One irrepressible Navajo relates some of his early experiences:

> In our field training, we had wires strung all over the place with guys sitting here and over there. We'd send messages, and the brass would be walking around and they would sneak over to the other end of our wires to see if the message was coming out the same as it went in. Then they'd send a runner back to see if the message sent and received were the same. They'd say, "I don't know how the hell they're doin' it." They'd hide us so we couldn't see each other while we were sending messages.
>
> Then those intelligence men recorded some of our messages and took them back to their offices to decode. They sat around three weeks trying to break them down and couldn't do it. Of course we could break down those messages in three shakes.
>
> We trained from ground to air and the messages still came out the same; and still the brass couldn't understand how we did it.

Of the original twenty-nine, two were retained at the training center as recruiters and instructors (John Benally and Johnny Manuelito) and the other twenty-seven were shipped out to Guadalcanal to initiate the use of the code in the combat area.

One of the men tells the story of their reception on the island in his humorous way:

31

We got to Guadalcanal with our orders to assist by code talking. We were supposed to take our orders to the general, but he was hard to find. He was 'way back of the lines. We were supposed to identify ourselves and turn over our orders. He just sat there and didn't say anything. We went back to the colonel who, I think, was Chief of Staff, and I told him what the deal was.

Finally he sent two guys over to the 1st, two to the 7th, two to the 11th, and two to the 5th regiments. Now we had gotten there about four o'clock in the morning, but we didn't get to talk any until nine o'clock at night. Then we were given permission to talk a little. I called the 7th Marines and before we finished talking, the radio was buzzing, the telephone was ringing, and then runners came to say that the Japs were talking on our frequency and that they had taken over everything, and that nobody could tell what the hell they were saying. The colonel tried to explain that our men [Navajos] were talking.

Well, he didn't know whether to send us back or leave us there. He mumbled, "You guys are more trouble than you're worth." I was sitting there nice and cozy, and now I had to go tell the guys that we wouldn't be using our code—at least for a while, to avoid panic in the ranks.

Then the colonel had an idea. He said he would keep us on one condition: that I could out-race his "white code"—a cylinder-thing that you set a coded message on and send by radio . . . tick, tick, tick. Then the receiver signals he has received the message and gives the roger on it. We both sent messages—with the white cylinder and by voice. Both of us received answers. The race was to see who could decode his answer first. He said, "Are you ready?" I said, "I've started already." "How long will it take you?" I was asked. "Two hours?" "Two hours? I can get ready in two minutes . . . and give you a head start," I answered.

I got the roger on my return message from four units in about four and a half minutes. The other guy was still decoding when I said, "Colonel, when are you going to give up that signal outfit? The Navajos are more efficient."

He didn't say anything, just started lighting up his pipe

and walked away. He was still scratching his head, wondering how we had exchanged messages so fast. I called to him, "Why don't you throw the thing away?" The Colonel answered, "You people throw away your papers or whatever you learned from, and *walk around, a Code!*"

This demonstration established the use of Navajo teams as a great adjunct to that of already functioning communications personnel.

Chapter Five

EXPANSION OF THE CODE

...A weird succession of guttural sounds.

Philip Johnston visited Camp Elliott frequently to check on the progress of the project (although he had nothing whatever to do with the formation of the code) and was elated with what he found there.

Some time after the code was well under way, he called on Colonel Jones at his home in San Diego, at which time he was informed that another request for 200 recruits had been sent to Washington. "This time I believe we're going to get them," Colonel Jones exclaimed jubilantly.

On hearing this optimistic report, Mr. Johnston (who was in his forties) asked timidly, "Colonel, if that authorization comes through, do you think you could use my services? I want to enlist if the Marine Corps will have me."

The colonel was delighted with Mr. Johnston's offer and confessed, "I never dreamed you'd want to come into the service. I'm sure we can get the necessary waivers for your age. We'd be more than happy to put you in charge of the training program."

Mr. Johnston recalls that "enroute to Los Angeles and home, my car seemed to float through a pink haze." But each subsequent day passed slowly as a week, and the slide-rule became heavy as lead. At last a letter came from Colonel Jones, stating that unlimited recruiting of Navajos had been authorized. He also suggested that Mr. Johnston write a personal letter to the Commandant, requesting permission to enlist "with noncommissioned rank, commensurate with duties assigned."

Technical Sergeant Philip Johnston, October, 1944.

On September 14, Mr. Johnston sent in his application for enlistment in the Marine Corps Reserve, Class 5-B, Specialist, "to serve in the capacity of training and direction of Navajo Indian personnel for communication, and to perform duty with them, both inside and outside the limits of the continental United States."

He wrote, "Because of my great desire to be of service in the foregoing capacity, and to get started in this work at the earliest possible moment, I am applying for enlistment in the Marine Corps rather than for a commission which would entail more time and uncertainty." (See Appendix, Item III.)

Already committed to the program involving the Navajo code by official authorization for unlimited recruiting, officials acted swiftly. Within a week, quartermaster personnel in San Diego were outfitting the elated Mr. Johnston with the uniform of a staff sergeant in the United States Marine Corps.

The plan for the use of Navajo Indians in the Signal Corps of the Marines, proposed in February, was now a reality; and the man who had fathered the *idea* had been put in charge of training—early in October.

After the departure of the twenty-seven men of the pilot project for Guadalcanal, John Benally and Johnny Manuelito were sent to the reservation to seek out new personnel for the communications program. They worked the Navajo area with Anglo recruiters, beginning in the autumn of 1942, with Mr. Benally working in the western half and Mr. Manuelito in the eastern half. Occasionally they joined forces in the same area, depending on where most of the prospective recruits were to be found. Early in 1943, they were reassigned back to the San Diego area.

Sergeant Johnston taught the first class of Navajo recruits in December, basing his instruction on the established code (formulated by the initial twenty-nine men). He taught only one class, then selected five men who seemed to be the most adept and proficient in communications, those who would

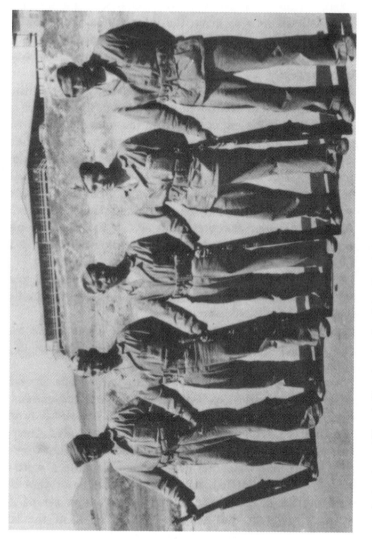

Instructors at Navajo Communication School Training Center, Camp Pendleton, 1943: John Manuelito, John Benally, Rex Kontz, Howard Billiman and Peter Tracy.

maintain the best relationship with other men, and those who were temperamentally suited to carry on the instruction under his supervision. He always knew who the men in the next class would be, for he was given the information from the boot camp where the men were in training. Sergeant Johnston left the area of instruction and gave his time thereafter to administration.

During the formulation of the basic code, Captain Stilwell, cryptographer, had monitored transmissions and offered criticisms. Since words not contained in the vocabulary had to be spelled out with the Navajo words for letters of the alphabet, Captain Stilwell felt that too many repetitions were necessarily introduced. For example, study the word *Guadalcanal,* which spelled with the word-alphabet becomes Goat-Ute-Ant-Deer-Ant-Lamb-Cat-Ant-Nut-Ant-Lamb. The four *Ants* might quickly be decoded as representing *A's* . . . that is, if the interpreter could understand Navajo. (Repetition of letters is one of the keys to deciphering any code.)

A second criticism was that, since spelling proper names and other terms without equivalents in the code was too time-consuming, additions were needed.

It was, therefore, decided to add 200 terms to the vocabulary, and provide alternate terms for the 12 letters of the alphabet most frequently repeated in English.

It was comparatively easy to come up with words representing various countries: *Rolled Hat* for Australia, *Bounded by Water* for Britain, *Braided Hair* for China, *Beard* for France, *Iron Hat* for Germany, *White Clothes* for India, *Red Army* for Russia and *Slant-Eyed* for Japan. These and others were decided upon; but when the group had to choose a word for Italy, they were baffled. Mr. Johnston said later that *Boot* (denoting the shape of the country) would have served as a perfect equivalent, but no one thought of it at the time. Finally, one Navajo said, "I knew an Italian once who couldn't talk without stuttering," so the word for Italy became *Stutter.*

In talking about this new list of words, one man says, "If

the word *Ant* appeared several times for *A*, and the enemy heard 'Wollachee, wollachee, wollachee,' he might catch on." So the group decided to add *Apple* (belasana), and *Axe* (tsen-hil), and so on.

The six letters most frequently repeated in the English language are E T A O I N. Alternates chosen for these letters are:

Elk	Turkey	Ant	Owl	Ice	Nut
Eye	Tea	Apple	Onion	Itch	Needle
Ear	Tooth	Axe	Oil	Intestine	Nose

The second set of letters most frequently used are S H R D L U. One alternate was adopted for each of these:

Sheep	Horse	Rabbit	Deer	Lamb	Ute
Snake	Hair	Ram	Dog	Leg	Uncle

The recruits were carefully trained in the use of the alternates. Captain Stilwell monitored the transmissions of messages, including the additions, and was completely satisfied.

Transmission speed (because of the addition of the 200 terms) had greatly increased, and the frequency of repeated letters had been corrected. *Guadalcanal* could now be spelled: Goat-Ute-Ant-Deer-Apple-Lamb-Cat-Axe-Nut-Axe-Leg.

The alphabet (with additional equivalents) and additions to vocabulary, plus terms for names of countries follow:

Alphabet

A	(Wol-la-chee)	Ant
A	(Be-la-sana)	Apple
A	(Tse-nihl)	Axe
B	(Shush)	Bear
C	(Moasi)	Cat
D	(Be)	Deer
D	(Lha-cha-eh)	Dog
E	(Dzeh)	Elk
E	(Ah-nah)	Eye

E	(Ah-jah)	Ear
F	(Ma-e)	Fox
G	(Klizzie)	Goat
H	(Lin)	Horse
H	(Tse-gah)	Hair
I	(Tkin)	Ice
I	(Yeh-hes)	Itch
I	(A-chi)	Intestines
J	(Tkele-cho-gi)	Jackass
K	(Klizzie-yassie)	Kid
L	(Dibeh-yassie)	Lamb
L	(Ah-jad)	Leg
M	(Na-as-tso-si)	Mouse
N	(Nesh-chee)	Nut
N	(Ts-a)	Needle
N	(A-chen)	Nose
O	(Ne-ahs-jah)	Owl
O	(Tlo-chin)	Onion
O	(A-kha)	Oil
P	(Bi-so-dih)	Pig
Q	(Ca-yeilth)	Quiver
R	(Gah)	Rabbit
R	(Dah-nas-tsa)	Ram
S	(Dibeh)	Sheep
S	(Klesh)	Snake
T	(Than-zie)	Turkey
T	(D-ah)	Tea
T	(A-woh)	Tooth
U	(No-da-ih)	Ute
U	(Shi-da)	Uncle
V	(A-keh-di-glini)	Victor
W	(Gloe-ih)	Weasel
X	(Al-an-as-dzoh)	Cross
Y	(Tash-as-zih)	Yucca
Z	(Besh-do-gliz)	Zinc

Names of countries:

Africa	Zhin-ni	Blackies
Alaska	Beh-hga	With winter
America	Ne-he-mah	Our mother
Australia	Cha-yes-desi	Rolled hat
Britain	Toh-ta	Bounded by water
China	Ceh-yehs-besi	Braided hair
France	Da-gha-hi	Beard
Germany	Besh-be-cha-he	Iron hat
Iceland	Tsin-ke-yah	Ice land

India	Ah-le-gai	White clothes
Italy	Doh-ha-chi-yali-tchi	Stutter
Japan	Beh-na-ali-tsoisi	Slant-eyed
Philippines	Ke-yah-da-na-ilhe	Floating land
Russia	Sila-go-che-ih	Red army
South America	Sha-de-ah-ne-he-mah	South-our mother
Spain	Deba-de-nih	Sheep-pain

General vocabulary:

About	Wola-chi-a-he-gahn	Ant fight
Activity	Ah-ha-tinh	Action ending with y
Adequate	Beh-gha	Enough or sufficient
Adjacent	Be-gahi	Near or close to
Adjust	Has-tai-nel-kad	Adjust
Affirmative	Lanh	Agree
After	Bi-kha-di	After
Ammunition	Beh-eli-doh-be-cah-ali-tas-ah	All sorts of shells
Angle	Dee-cahn	Slanting
Announce	Beh-ha-o-dze	Announce
Anti-aircraft	Tsisi-be-wol-doni	Bird-shooter
Anti-tank	Chay-ta-gahi-be-wol-doni	Tortoise-shooter
Any	Tah-ha-dah	Any
Appear	Ye-ka-ha-ya	Appear
Approximately	To-kus-dan	Approximately
Assembly	De-ji-kash	Bunch together
Assign	Bah-deh-tahn	Give
Astride	Yi-nas-kai	Astride
At	Ah-di	At
Attack	Al-tah-je-jay	Attack
Attention	Goha	Attention
Authorize	Be-b-ho-snee	Authorize
Baggage	Khailh	Load
Battle	Da-ah-hi-dzi-sit	Battle
Beach	Tah-bahn	Beach
Between	Bi-tah-kiz	Between
Bivouac	Ehl-nas-teh	Brush shelter
But	Neh-dihn-di	But
Cannot	Yah-de-zini-do-ta	Cannot
Carry	Yo-lailh	Carry
Case	Bit-sah	Case
Cause	Bi-nih-nani	Cause
Cavalry	Lin-yea-nal-dai-hi	Horsemen
Ceiling	Da-tel-jay	Seal
Center	Ulh-ne-ih	Center

Change	Thla-go-a-nat-zah	Change
Chemical	Ta-nee	Alkali
Circuit	Ah-heh-ha-dailh	Circuit
Clear	Yo-ah-hol-zhod	Clear
Close	Ul-chi-un-nal-yah	Close
Come	Huc-quo	Come
Commercial	Nai-el-ne-hi	Commercial
Communication	Ha-neh-al-enji	Making talk
Communique	Hane-el-ini	Communique
Consist	Beh	With
Contact	Ah-hi-di-dail	Come together
Control	Nai-ghiz	Control
Consolidate	Ah-hih-hi-nil	Put together
Continue	Ta-yi-teh	Continue
Course	Coh-ji-goh	This way
Cross	Al-n-as-dzoh	Cross
Dash	Us-dzoh	Dash
Dawn	Ha-yeli-kahn	Early morning
Degree	Nahl-kihd	Move around
Delay	Be-sitihn	Deer lay
Deliver	Be-bih-zihde	Deer liver
Demolition	Ah-deel-tahi	Blow up
Depart	Da-de-yah	He left
Designate	Ye-khi-del-nei	Point out
Detached	Al-cha-nil	Detached
Detail	Be-beh-sha	Deer tail
Dig in	Le-eh-gade	Dig in
Direction	Ah-ji-go	Direction
Distribute	Nah-neh	Issue
District	Be-thin-ya-ni-che	Deer ice strict
Driven	Ah-nol-kahl	Driven
Each	Tal-lahi-ne-zini-go	Each
Edge	Bi-ba-hi	Edge
Effective	Bi-delh-need	Effective
Effort	Yea-go	With all your might
Element	Ah-na-nai	Troops representing others
Elevation	Ali-khi-ho-ne-oha	Elevation
Eliminate	Ha-boh-do-dzil	Eliminate
Emergency	Ho-nez-cla	Emergency
Encircle	Ye-nas-teh (with S)	Surround
Encounter	Bi-khanh	Go against
Engage	A-ha-ne-ho-ta	Agreed
Entire and all	Ta-a-tah	All
Envelop	A-zah-gi-ya	Surround
Equipment	Ya-ha-de-tahi	Equipment
Erection	Yeh-zihn	Stand up
Evacuate	Ha-na	Move out

Exchange	Alh-nahl-yah	Exchange
Executive	Beh-da-hol-nehi	Those in charge
Failure	Yees-ghin	Failure
Farm	Mai-he-ahgan	Fox-arm
Force	Ta-na-ne-lailh	Without care
Form	Bi-cha	Form
Formation	Bi-cha-ye-lailh	Formation
Fortification	An-na-sozi	Cliff dwelling
Forward	Tehi	Let's go
Friendly	Neh-hecho-da-nai	Friendly
From	Bi-tsan-dehn	From
Furnish	Yeas-nil	Furnish
Further	Wo-nas-di	Further
Guide	Nah-o-thlai	Guide
Hall	Lhi-ta-a-ta	Horse all
Halt	Ta Akwai-i	Halt
Handle	Bet-seen	Handle
Held	Wo-tah-ta-eh-dahn-oh	Hold (past tense)
High	Wo-tah	Up
Highway	Wo-dah-ho-ho-ne-teh	High way
Hold	Wo-tgan	Hold
Hostile	A-nah-ne-dzin	Not friendly
Howitzer	Be-el-ton-tso-quodi	Short big gun
Impact	A-he-dis-goh	Impact
Important	Ba-has-teh	Important
Improved	Ho-dol-zhond	Improved
Include	El-tsod	Include
Increase	Ho-nalh	Increase
Indicate	Ba-hal-neh	Tell about
Infantry	Ta-neh-nal-dahi	Infantry
Initial	Beh-ed-de-dlid	Brand
Installation	Nas-nil	In place
Instruct	Na-ne-tgin	Teach
Intense	Dzeel	Strength
Interfere	Ah-nilh-khlai	Interfere
Investigate	Na-ali-ka	Track
Involve	A-tah	Involve
Kettle	Jah-ho-loni	Dutch oven
Killed	Naz-tsaid	Killed
King	Olah-bi-chuh-hi	Gold hat wearer
Knot	Shazh	Knot
Lade	Hea-le	Load (baggage)
Land	Kay-yah	Land
Least	De-be-yazie-ha-a-ah	Lamb east
Leave	Dah-de-yah	Lamb depart
Less	Bi-oh	Less
Liaison	Da-a-he-gi-neh	Know other's action

Loss	Ut-din	Loss
Manage	Hastni-beh-naphai	Man-age
Maximum	Bil-dil-khon	Fill to top
Mechanized elements	Chidi-da-ah-he-goni	Fighting cars
Medical	A-zay	Medicine
Merchant ship	Na-el-nehi-tsin-na-ailh	Merchant ship
Minute	Ah-khay-el-kit-yazzie	Little hour
Mission	Ai-neshodi	Mission
Mistake	O-zhi	Miss
More	Thla-na-nah	More
Motion	Na-hot-nah	Motion
Motor	Chide-be-tse-tsen	Car head
Net	Na-nes-tizi	Net
Neutral	Do-neh-lini	Neutral
Normal	Doh-a-ta-ha-dah	Normal
Notice	Ne-da-tazi-thin	No-turkey-ice
Obstacle	Da-ho-dosh-zha	Obstacle
Once	Ta-lai-di	Once
Only	Ta-ei-tay-a-yah	Only
Operate	Ye-nahl-nish	Work at
Opportunity	Ash-ga-alin	Opportunity
Other	La-e-gih	Other
Out	Clo-dih	Out doors
Over	Ba-ha-this	Over
Paratroopers	No-pahl-yeh-nal-tehi	Canvas troopers
Particular	A-yo-ad-do-neh	Particular
Party	Da-sha-jah	Group
Pay	Na-eli-ya	Pay
Percent	Yal	Corruption: "real" spelling
Plane	Tsidi	Bird
Position	Bilh-has-ahn	Position
Post	Sah-dei	Post
Prepare	Hash-tay-ho-dit-ne	Prepare
Present	Cut	Now
Probable	Da-tsi	Maybe
Provide	Yis-nil	Furnish
Quick	Shil-loh	Quick
Raid	Dez-jay	Raid
Rate	Gah-eh-yahn	Rabbit-ate
Ready	Khut	Now
Rear	Be-ka-denh	Behind
Recommend	C he-ho-dai-tahn	Recommend
Refire	Na-na-coh	Again fire
Regulate	Na-yel-na	Regulate
Relief	Aganh-tol-jay	Relief

Reorganize	Ha-dit-zah	Reorganize
Reserve	Hesh-j-e	Reserve
Resist	Tahn-col-ehi	Resist
Restrict	Be-ho-chinh	Restrict
Within	Bilh-bigih	Within
Without	Ta-gaid	Without
Wood	Chis	Fire wood or woods
Wounded	Cah-da-khi	Wounded
Yard	A-del-tahl	Step
Zero	Nos-bas	Round

After memorizing the alphabet equivalents, and practicing spelling out terms and names of places, the Navajo recruits then set about the prodigious task of memorizing the entire vocabulary of 411 terms. Memory had to be lightning fast in a combat situation.

Mr. Johnston says, "The code talkers presented a phenomenal feat of memory, and I don't know to this day how they could react so quickly to those substitute words in Navajo in a fraction of a second. To arrive at this proficiency, they had to study long hours—day and night." He reports that the drill continued over portable radios in the field day after day and "deft fingers trained in rapid legible printing recorded those messages." Washington officials never ceased to be amazed at the dispatches that materialized from a "weird succession of guttural, nasal, tongue-twisting sounds."

One of the Indian instructors reports that camp was not made up of eight-hour days. He says:

We'd spend the day on field exercises, crawling around, and walking with walkie-talkies. It was hard on our men, but we studied long hours at night. When Mr. Johnston, who acted as the bridge between the Navajos and the Marine Corps for the duration would ask, "What do you think of Mr. So and So? Do you think he'll make it?" I knew I didn't have any business saying that Mr. So and So *would* make it as a Navajo communicator, unless I knew in my heart he had the capability. Just because I liked the way he looked and because we got on well together was not enough. I had

45

to know that man would qualify, that he was going to be faithful to his dying breath. Then I could say, "Yes." We weeded out and turned down some of our Navajos because they had to have a certain education—let's say tenth grade. They had to be able to spell words like *reconnaissance.*

There were those who wanted to be code talkers who weren't Navajos—children of traders. They had been born on the reservation, had been brought up with the Indian children, but the language they knew was what we called the "trading post language" and they were not able to carry on an intelligent conversation in Navajo. They could only say "Flour, sugar, coffee" and "Hello, my friend. How are you?" Little more. They just could not do what the Navajos and Marines had set up as a combined effort to accomplish. We tested some of them but decided they were not capable of handling the work. We'd send them to motor transport or the infantry. We could not use them where there were thousands and thousands of lives at stake. If anyone would make the mistake of chalking down one digit incorrectly, saying, "We are strafing, shelling or bombing Position XX, Number so and so," and it would be sent as *1000 yards,* instead of *100 yards*, you might get strafing, bombing and shelling your own men. We couldn't take that chance.

Every syllable in the Navajo language means something, and has to be pronounced exactly right. So we had to turn away those non-Navajos who were proficient in the trading post language only.

This was a highly selected group. I had to be able to talk to a man and say, "I want you to get on that hill, and I'm going to give you so many messages and then after I have given you the last message, act according to that message. Understand? Is that clear?" If the man would nod, that didn't mean anything. He had to say, "Yes, sir!" with a quick snap. Then if I had any reason to doubt the voice, I'd ask, "Why do you answer me that way? Why can't you answer 'Yes, sir'? Tell me!" The man might then say, "Well, will you go over that just once more?" That was just what I thought. When the men understood they would repeat the orders to me. They had to get it down *pat*, so I would know it was right!

This instructor says that not all of the code talkers had the same I.Q. Some caught on a great deal faster than others. The slower group would then stay in training a little longer to master the code.

Some time after the code talkers entered active service, Colonel Tinsley asked the regimental commander how he could be sure that the message one gave was the one received. After all, the Indians had no word for *mortar,* for they had never had such a weapon at the reservation. The answer was, "You can't be sure, but the messages get through!" Then he added, "I happen to know that the Indian word for *mortar* is *gun that squats* (or *sitting gun*)." Colonel Tinsley says, "With that as a sample, one can imagine how garbled a message might sound to the white man."

The recruiting of Navajos on the reservation was accelerated and enough men were signed up to sustain the training program on a regular basis. However, to spur the continued search for qualified Navajos, Sergeant Johnston set up a document outlining plans for speeding the process.

He pointed out that authority had been granted by the Commandant to recruit 200 Navajos qualified for work as communications personnel, but that far less than that number had enlisted. He stated that although the Navajo tribe numbered about 50,000, the percentage of illiteracy was high, and that efforts to procure a sufficient number for communications duty would entail an intensive canvass of schools, a scrutiny of selective service registration rolls, and a diligent search for qualified individuals both on the reservation and in adjacent towns where some had found employment.

He proposed that a mobile unit be formed for recruiting purposes, with a commissioned officer in charge, assisted by a clerk and a Navajo Marine, and if possible a doctor to make physical examinations without delay. (See Appendix, Item IV.)

That same month, Mr. Johnston sent a letter of inquiry to Major Shannon of the Marine Recruiting Station in Phoenix, that throws some light on the success of the code talkers who were seeing action in combat areas, and Mr. Johnston's desire for more men for the program.

Navajo Communication School
Training Center
Camp Elliott, San Diego, California

22 February 1943

Major Frank L. Shannon
Marine Corps Recruiting Station
222 Security Building
Phoenix, Arizona

Dear Major Shannon:

The Navajo Communication School has been under my supervision since formal classes were opened on 7 December last. Progress has been excellent, and men who have completed the course are fully qualified to transmit orders and messages accurately in their native tongue.

The value of Navajo communication personnel has already been demonstrated in the South Pacific Area. A booklet issued by the War office entitled "Fighting on Guadalcanal" contains the following statement: "We have two American Indians we use as 'talkers' on the telephone or voice radio when we want to transmit secret or important messages." A communication from General Vandergrift to the Commandant dated 3 December 1942, requests the assignment of eighty-three Navajos to various units of the First Marines for communication duty.

It is my understanding that all recruiting of Navajos was discontinued some time ago, but that provision has been made for bringing them into the Marine Corps through the Selective Service. I shall greatly appreciate such information as you may be able to give relative to present plans for assigning Navajo personnel to our branch of the service for training in communication.

Respectfully yours,

_____

Philip Johnston
S-Sgt., USMCR

An intensive search for additional Navajo personnel followed, and the training program continued with a number of classes receiving simultaneous instruction at the base.

One day at Camp Elliott, Sergeant Johnston received an order to see the chief of staff. On reporting, he was handed correspondence between the chief of staff's office and that of the Commandant in Washington, stating that inasmuch as the Navajos there at the communications school had a high intelligence quotient, a good education, and a command of two languages, they should be recommended for the rank of private first class at the completion of their training. This was to be an incentive for the men, to show them that the Corps was grateful for what they were doing. The men responded as expected—with even more enthusiasm for the job they were doing.

Early in 1943, the Navajo training center was moved to Camp Pendleton, about thirty miles up the coast from San Diego, where it remained for the duration of the war. It was here at a crucial time in the training of six or seven classes, only one week before graduation, that the order for raise in rank was rescinded. Each Navajo expected to receive the rank of private first class—a rank that under ordinary circumstances might not be achieved in less than a year's commendable service.

Captain Conner, later on Major Conner, the adjutant and signal officer for the Fifth Division, called Sergeant Johnston into his office to tell him that Colonel Jones of Camp Elliott (the school's former headquarters), who had the responsibility of approving all nominations for raise in rank, had been transferred to another post and his place had been taken by a Colonel Creswell. Colonel Creswell had disapproved all the names of the graduates of the classes in the Navajo training center. He had said, "I have some candidates of my own who will get preference."

Major Sullivan, commanding officer, tried to change Colonel Creswell's mind, because these men had been promised the rank, and he felt very deeply that the promise was sacred and should be kept. He assured Colonel Creswell that no further promises for the rank would be made to new recruits entering the program.

Although Major Sullivan presented his case eloquently, he was informed in sharp terms by Colonel Creswell that he wanted to hear no more about it. Captain Conner reported the ultimatum to Sergeant Johnston and told him to get the men in formation and he would tell them the bad news. The sergeant, however, insisted, "It's a dirty job, but it's mine and I'll do it."

The innate strength of character and acceptance of what cannot be helped was reflected in the reaction of the Navajo communicators; they evidenced no outward sign of disappointment or ill feeling, earning for themselves the deep gratitude of their officers at the camp.

Marines at Navajo Communication School Training Center, Camp Pendleton, 1943.

Chapter Six

THE NAVAJO CODE TALKERS IN ACTION

... The eyes and ears of the world are on you!

Anglo Marine Louis Steinbacher tells a humorous story concerning the Navajo code talkers early in the war. Preceding the invasion of Roi-Namur in the Marshalls, he was aboard the navy ship GC-1 *Appalachian* (a communications ship loaded with radio transmitters, receivers and antennae)—the flagship of Admiral Richard L. Conolly, commander Task Force Northern Expeditionary Troops. While en route to Roi-Namur, orders were given to break radio silence by opening up with every radio aboard, sending "dummy" messages. This, they were told, was to make the enemy think that an enormous armada of ships was heading out. The most powerful radio set on the ship, an army SCR-299, was mounted in a panel truck, parked on the highest deck of the ship. The operation had no more than gotten started when General Quarters sounded on board ship. Sailors ran to their battle stations expecting an attack; but after a while all was secured and activities returned to normal.

This is the story they were told later: The ship's own radio picked up the Navajos' fake messages. The navy operators, hearing the foreign tongue coming in so loud, thought it was the whole Japanese fleet right over the horizon. The commanding officer evidently informed the proper authorities of the code talkers on board, and the admiral had requested to hear the Indians in action.

In his book, *Guadalcanal Diary,* Richard Tregaskis writes:

The ship was approaching Guadalcanal, and it was the night before. Dr. Malcolm V. Pratt, the senior medical officer aboard told the author this amusing story: "I went below to look around in the hole last night, expecting to find the kids praying, and instead I found 'em doing a war dance. One of them had a towel for a loincloth and a blacked face, and he was doing a cancan while another beat a tomtom."[4]

After a landing, the Marines usually cut a swath three or four feet wide into the tangled jungle, broad enough for ammunition carts to pass through. They were often able to penetrate thousands of yards within two hours after the first landing wave hit the beach—confounding the grateful army contingents that followed.

The signalmen set up the tall antennae of their field radio at the side of the trail, then tied the generator to a tree and cranked it. One of the original twenty-seven code talkers on Guadalcanal relates the procedure as follows:

We used several types of radio sets. The TBX unit was the one that we used most. It weighed about 80 pounds—very heavy to lug around. We had two sets: a transmitter and a receiver, connected with junky cable. We tried to set the generator on a bench of some kind when we could, so we could straddle the bench and crank the thing. But this didn't work on a location where it was sandy. So the coconut tree came in very handy. We hooked the generator to the trunk, straddled the tree and cranked. It took two men— one to crank the generator and get the juice going into the mike, and the other to transmit the message. We got information off the ship [the transport] after a landing, and kept those in charge of the operation informed.

One thing we learned in school was not to be on the air longer than was absolutely necessary. We had to be careful not to repeat words in a sentence—that is, if the message had to go through more than once, we tried to say it dif-

4. Richard Tregaskis, *Guadalcanal Diary*, New York: Random House, 1943, p. 32.

ferently every time. We were also told not to use the same word too often in a sentence, and that we had to be *accurate* the first time! If a message has to be corrected or repeated too often, you are giving the enemy a better chance to locate you. On Guadalcanal we had to move our equipment in a hurry because the Japs started to shell the very spot where we were operating.

In reminiscing about his experiences in the field as a code talker, one of the men said, "I was with the forward CP when we ran out of ammunition and there were many wounded to be evacuated. I sent messages asking for medical call, supplies and food." He added, "I didn't have any 'pet' way of sending messages such as some teams cooked up—making up stories with messages in them. Messages in the code were sent just as fast as though we were talking directly in one language such as English."

The men did regular Marine duty much of the time but were available for communication work at all times. One reports, "We might be 100 to 200 yards away when somebody would run to us and say, 'A Navajo message!' Then we'd hurry to our equipment to receive the message. The way it was known that there was a message in Navajo is that the word 'Arizona' or 'New Mexico' was used to indicate that one of us was needed."

The use of the code was totally at the discretion of the commanding officer, of course. Interviews with code talkers who were active in the campaign in the South Pacific disclose the fact that their service to their officers varied greatly. Some officers used the code almost exclusively when they were in "tight" situations, while others report that their officers relied on other means of transmitting messages at such times.

Lieutenant General R. E. Cushman, Jr., says, "It seems to me that the code talkers were used mostly in communications from battalion to company level, wherein the tendency was to give away a lot of information if the conversation was in English."

54

Lieutenant General (Ret.) A. L. Bowser, who served with the Third Division, remembers using the Navajos for classified messages to the regiments when the radio was out—which was frequent in the jungle country. He recalls that for some reason the 21st Marines used them more than other outfits.

Colonel C. A. Laster says that the Navajo code was not needed in areas "where the officers felt that the Japanese were not in a position locally to monitor or react to regimental or battalion tactical nets."

Marlowe Williams (who served as battalion commander during the Guam campaign) had a code talker assigned to him for sending messages during landings and beach assaults. He says,

> I recall that this talker was very helpful in my CP group in providing radio transmissions and vital information for the establishment of the initial CP location (the location selected pre-D-day being untenable) and all through in an Indian language, which to my knowledge was never intercepted or decoded.

One Navajo feels that the commanding officers did not recognize the value of the code at first, but by the time the Fourth Division was in action, it had become a "more or less established system and was used quite a lot." He said the code had become somewhat "perfected" by this time.

Some officers used the talkers a great deal in rear echelons but it was sometimes necessary to utilize the men in landings and in front lines with their portable equipment. Telephones could not be used until after lines had been established, of course. One of the men reports that they did not always have the same teammates, exchanging at times in the battle area. Some of those in the front lines used Morse code and radio with straight messages in English, as well as sending them in the code. Messages were sometimes sent simultaneously in the different media.

He feels the code was very effective in spotting artillery or directing shelling. The area was marked off in squares and numbered. A directive might be: "Artillery needed 265." In such a situation, the Navajo language was most effective because it was done so fast. Forward observers would spot these areas and give the information to the talkers for transmission.

He remembers one place where they had the code down so "pat" that the Navajo at the other end said, "They are going to have a squaw dance in quad 11. Stand by. Birds are coming." (Birds were fighter planes, of course, and the dive bomber a chicken hawk.) It sounded as if they were planning to have a lot of fun in quad 11; but the message told the code talker that the enemy would be bombing there. The most important use of the coded messages (or so it seemed to this Navajo) was pinpointing areas that were in danger.

Many of the Navajos report that, according to their experiences, the code was extremely helpful when things were tight (which they often were)—such as on approaching the islands. During a coordinated assault (with perhaps the Australians, Marines and the United States Army Force making the attack simultaneously) fast communication was imperative. The Navajo code was much more quickly translated than any of the other codes in use.

Another code talker reports that his officers used the code more often when things were more relaxed, rather than when they were "tight." He says,

I remember very well the campaign on Saipan, when we wanted to take a town "standing up." But the Japs had moved a lot of their guns into the town, and they started lobbing everything they had at us. So the navy was given the order to level the town. We circled it. We were relieved by army personnel who set up positions in front of us. But that night the Japs launched the biggest counterattack of the Saipan campaign. They broke through the army line and we had to form another line. Actually we didn't know which was the Jap line and which was our own army line. There we were in the dark all night long in that precarious situation. The Japs captured some of our artillery, but they had no ammunition so it was useless to them. But of course *we* didn't have it then, and that was pretty sad. Two days later we finished off at the island and pulled across to Tinian.

Very little code talking was possible during this emergency on Saipan because things were moving too fast. It seems to me that the use of the code was most effective when the Marines were up against something—when we were sitting in one place too long, and wanted to move on. When lines were established and planned strategy could be carried out—to take the next hill, the airport or what have you—that's when the code talkers were in greatest demand.

It is reported that the need for the code was not as great during the invasion of the Marshall Islands as for some of the others, for these were not as well fortified, and landings and assault were not as difficult and hazardous.

At Tinian (in the Marianas) the communication crews rotated on duty around the clock.

One Navajo was on a sub-chaser on the way to Saipan and he reports that during the trip he was in constant communication with all ships in the convoy; however, he had little to do because they didn't encounter the enemy on the trip. They dug foxholes soon after they landed on Saipan, because the Japanese hit the beach with fire. As soon as it was possible, they set up communications, even though they were still being shelled. Fortunately, shrapnel did not hit the radio. When they got to the "top" they were amazed that they had made it alive, for they could see that they had been "sitting ducks" for the enemy.

"Voice code transmissions of operational orders laid groundwork for advances from the Solomons straight through Okinawa,"[5] says the writer of an article for *The Leatherneck*. For example, the Naval Air Force ran into stiff resistance around the Bismarck Archipelago. It appeared that the Japanese were able to decode messages without difficulty and

5. Vernon Langille, "Indian War Call," *The Leatherneck*, vol. 31-A, March, 1948, p. 37.

so were apprized in advance of where the aerial forces would strike. The pilots' name for Rabaul, "Dead End," was well deserved. Many a flyer was lost over the landlocked harbor, a victim of murderous anti-aircraft guns placed on surrounding hills, pouring death-dealing fire at bombers winging their way through "The Slot."

But eleven code talkers brought in to man the navy air net secured the communications, preventing the enemy from acquiring knowledge of intended attacks ahead of time. These Navajos were "life savers" in every sense of the word.

Back at camp, Sergeant Johnston, still alarmed because the procurement of Navajo personnel was falling below the goal of 25 a month, sent a suggestion to the Commandant of the United States Marine Corps, proposing that a center be set up in the South Pacific for training Navajos already in the service. He wrote that the proposal had been made to recruit and train Navajo "talkers" in the Marine Corps in sufficient numbers to assign 82 to each division. Only 163 had enlisted at the time, 24 of whom had failed to make the grade.

To alleviate the shortage, Sergeant Johnston recommended that a skeleton crew of code talkers (six to eight men) be attached to each Marine Corps division to participate in tactical problems, and that the balance of Navajo personnel be assigned to a training center in the South Pacific area. He suggested that someone else might take his place at Camp Pendleton to free him for supervision of the training of new personnel in the Pacific.

Sergeant Johnston's suggestion was not acted upon for some time. Meanwhile, letters regarding the successful use of the Navajo code talkers in the field came to his attention, giving him further inspiration to press on with his project of training Indian communicators. On May 15 (1943) Julian C. Smith, commanding general of the Second Marine Division, Fleet Marine Force, in the field, wrote such a letter concerning the success of the project. He said (in part):

(a) In their primary billets as "talkers" they have functioned very well, handling traffic rapidly and accurately.
(b) When not employed as "talkers," some of the Navajos have been used as message center men, and some as radio operators. They have functioned satisfactorily in both capacities.
(c) As general duty Marines they have, in general, been excellent, showing above average willingness to work at any job assigned them.

He, therefore, recommended that the program of supplying Navajo Indians trained as "talkers" to Fleet Marine Force units be continued. (See Appendix, Item VI.)

In June, the commanding general of the First Amphibious Corps, in the field, urged the Commandant of the United States Marine Corps to encourage Navajos to continue to enlist in the Corps as communications personnel. He also suggested a plan of distribution of the men, after training. The heart of his communication follows:

1. It is considered desirable to continue enlisting Navajo Indians for duty in the Marine Corps as Communications Personnel.

2. The primary duties of these men should be that of "talkers" for transmitting messages in their own language over telephone circuits, as well as over radio circuits. Their secondary duties should be that of message center personnel (messengers). This designation will not limit their usefulness to the Marine Corps, however, as they have shown remarkable aptitude in the performance as general duty Marines.

3. The following table is a suggested distribution and is also believed to be minimum requirements:

2 per Infantry and artillery battalion
4 per Infantry and artillery regiment
4 per Engineer regiment
2 per Engineer battalion
8 per Pioneer battalion

4 per Amphibian tractor battalion
6 per special weapons battalion
6 per tank company
6 per scout company
8 per signal company
2 per parachute battalion
4 per parachute regiment
8 per raider battalion
6 per raider regiment
8 per corps signal battalion
8 per corps anti tank battalion
4 per corps 115m artillery battalion

(See Appendix, Item VII.)

By the end of August, 191 Navajos had enlisted in the communications program. At this time, Sergeant Johnston reaffirmed his belief that a training center should be established in the South Pacific area. This plan and his reasons for it are found in his letter of August 30 to the Commandant of the United States Marine Corps, in which he repeated his recommendation that a skeleton crew of qualified "talkers" be attached to each division and that the remainder of the Navajo personnel be assigned to a training center somewhere in the South Pacific area. He laid out the three-fold advantages of such a plan:

(a) Integration of Navajo personnel as one unit would overcome a tendency of detached groups to develop idiomatic usages of words and phrases which are variants from the primary instruction in military communication. . . . Continued practice alone can insure the speed and accuracy essential to military operations. . . .

(b) Combat experiences of Navajo personnel, together with criticisms and suggestions from officers who have made use of Navajo communication in the combat areas will comprise invaluable data to be added to instruction procedure.

(c) The shortage of Navajo personnel can at least be partially offset by a plan of rationing, under which a division about to enter a combat area would be allocated a sufficient number of "talkers" from the pool to man all voice radio circuits in the lower echelons which may be in close contact with the enemy.

Sergeant Johnston again appealed for selective service authorities to advise all draft boards in Arizona, New Mexico and southern California of the special need for educated Navajos in the Marine Corps, in order that such personnel, employed off the reservation in large numbers, might be assigned to the Marine Corps for communications duty. (See Appendix, Item VIII.)

Sergeant Johnston's suggestion was carried out in due time. A large number of talkers stationed throughout the Pacific, assembled in Hawaii, where they made revisions in the code, and added words to the vocabulary list. One of the talkers tells about the program in his division (the Fifth) this way:

It was decided to get all the code talkers together every month to tell them what changes had been made in the code. I was picked to make arrangements and send memos to all the code talkers in my division. I was told, "We'll find the place and then the men will all come together and you can instruct them, explaining the changes that have been made in the code. If you need another day, we can arrange for two days. Headquarters in Oahu is about two hundred miles away; you'll fly up there for two or three days ahead of time to get all the information you need."

So that was all arranged for me every month before we would have our meeting. I did this for four months. The same boys came from all over for these refresher courses. Some of the boys missed out because they were on maneuvers on the day set for the course. The boys suggested that all of them congregate for a longer time to give them the chance to rehearse the terms. When they rushed back to their companies, they were often sent out again on maneuvers and really did not use the code's new terms as much as they could have.

When I went back to camp I talked to my captain and

told him how the boys felt about the course—the need for a longer time. The captain was very reasonable about the new plan and within a week it was O.K.'d by headquarters. The code talkers of the Fifth Division came together as planned and stayed several weeks. When they were ready to go back to their companies they were very accurate, very sharp!

The Navajo who managed the retraining program in Hawaii reports an extremely humorous incident that surely made the Indians appear tougher than their white Marine buddies. This is the way he tells it:

We were training on the Hawaiian Islands on a two-day maneuver. The first lieutenant (we called him Stormy) said, "We're going to see how tough you guys are. We're going to cross this desert in two days. We're going to use only one canteen of water each, and we're going to see how well you can preserve that water." We started off. It was real hot. I imagine we walked about twenty miles that first day.

He gave orders that we were not to eat the prickly pear cactus, and said, "I don't know whether they are safe to eat or not, but we'll stay on the safe side, because we don't want anybody to get sick." Well, we Indians knew about that cactus. About three o'clock that first day, when Stormy wasn't watching, we went over and cut the tops off some prickly pears, cut them down, and sucked out the liquid. We didn't touch the water in our canteens. We didn't need it.

The next day we started out and actually walked about ten miles when all at once, everybody was fagged out. All the men had emptied their canteens and were dying of thirst. We'd shake our canteens and the men would say, "Oh ... HOW do you Indians get along without water?" We'd answer in an offhand manner, "Oh, we've got lots of water left."

About two o'clock they started keeling over. They just couldn't go any farther. So one of us Navajos said, "Let's go over to Stormy and see how tough he is." He was just sitting there on a hill. We said to him, "Come on! Let's go!"

"Do you fellows still have plenty of water?" he asked, and we said, "Oh yeah . . . we've got plenty of water," and we all shook our canteens so that he could hear the water gurgle. Then we said, "Come on! We've just got ten more miles to go to get out of the desert!"

He said, "I don't think I can make it. I'm out of water and I don't want to ask you fellows for any of yours." So we all just sat down. But he was game and didn't want to give up. Pretty soon he got up and said, "Now if there are any of you that think you can't make it, you stay right here and when we get back to camp, we'll have them send water out." We had gone about 100 yards when he fell down. This time he gave up and said, "I don't think I can go any farther." He lay down and everybody else did too, excepting us three Navajos and we were still standing up. Stormy said weakly, "Hey, Chiefs, do you think you can go all the way in and back to camp? I'm going to write a letter for you to give to Colonel Woods. This will tell him to fly out some water in a five-gallon can and drop it. And then get a water truck and tell him to come in tonight with more."

So we went on in and got into camp about five o'clock. I gave the note to Colonel Woods and he laughed. He asked me, "Why don't the men out there have any water?" I told him we were trying to get across the desert on that two-day hike on one canteen of water. "That's not right," he said. "You're supposed to have one canteen for each day."

Well, he did order planes to fly cans of water over there, but I heard that when they dropped they split wide open, and the men ran to the spot and lapped up the water like dogs. The truck was late getting there and those poor guys almost died of thirst. When it did arrive the men drank it all! I wouldn't wonder if it was 100 gallons.

We never told Stormy why we still had water in our canteens. I suppose he and the other guys thought, "Wow! Those Navajos are tough! No wonder they can live on the reservation. They can live without water!"

As has already been noted, the communicators were used as

63

troubleshooters as well as talkers. One of the men tells of one harrowing experience:

I was at the radio station when a man came from Company A. He was a new man, with the rank of corporal. He was to go with me to show the way to where the lines needed repair. I put the necessary wire on my hip and started running. Since the corporal was a new man, a lieutenant said he would go with us.

The corporal got lost. I knew he was lost and I said, "This is not the place we're supposed to go to." I stopped and pulled up in the canyon to see if I was wrong. Companies A, B and C were spread out in this area. As soon as I stepped into that canyon we were met with fire, so we moved back out as quickly as we could. But the corporal did not move quickly enough. We discovered we were on the wrong side of the company that needed the repair. We crawled back to our base and had to report that we had lost everything. We couldn't even bring back the body of the corporal.

I was told that Japanese in Marines' clothing were up front and that the Marines had fired on them. We had been fired upon by our own men! I felt so badly about it that I lost all my strength for a while.

When these troubleshooters had to go out during the night, they were met by guards with leveled guns (on their return) and the time-worn question, "Who's there?" or "Who's coming?" They had to know the password, which, in the case of the company of the man quoted above, was the name of any state in the union—New York, Wisconsin, Indiana, Virginia, or what have you.

During certain combat situations (like the one described previously in taking a town on Saipan) the code talkers found it impossible to send messages. Such a situation faced one special team of code talkers when they stormed ashore on Tarawa, in one of the bloodiest operations of the war. They were on one of the earliest waves and got too far into the front lines. The platoon commander kept pushing them to go

Indian Marines and their Guam "tepee." (*USMC*)

forward, and of course they obeyed, only to find they were caught directly in the crossfire. One of them dropped into a foxhole, and was surprised to find that he had company—a Japanese. He says he hoped and prayed he wouldn't be stabbed to death by the man, but he escaped death in the hole for a very good reason—the man was dead. The men of his platoon were pinned down for some time by enemy fire, but finally all was clear and they were able to get out of their critical position. After the company was able to assemble, the Navajos got together and compared stories. But—during all this time—under the very thumb of the enemy—no messages were sent. Headquarters just gave orders and the company followed them.

A white Marine relates a dramatic story concerning the service rendered by the code talkers. It was on Saipan when his battalion occupied a position on the division's extreme left. One night the enemy retreated to a new line several hundred yards to the rear, and a few hours later, the Marines advanced to the old positions previously held by the Japanese, when a salvo exploded nearby. They radioed headquarters, reminding them that Americans now held this position, but another salvo came over. It was then they "knew the score." Headquarters did not believe them. And why should they? The Japanese had imitated American broadcasts many times before. Again they were showered with mud from a salvo that came even closer. And then they heard the question from headquarters: "Do you have a Navajo?" The Marine says he will never forget the message that was sent by the single Navajo in the battalion, although he couldn't understand a word of it. A few minutes later he and his comrades saw a cloud of smoke rising from the Japanese positions. They had been saved from being "clobbered" by their own artillery—by that Navajo message.

The Japanese were very clever at communications interference, sending fake orders in excellent "American-English," and jamming frequencies.

American forces were amazed to discover the ability of the

Japanese to speak English without a trace of accent or Oriental inflection—but the mystery was partially solved when it was found that many of the dead Japanese wore American high school class rings, and that many of the officers were graduates of American universities.

One code talker says, "The Japanese used to get on our frequency and talk; so one night we heard the Japanese talking and they used a word exactly like the Navajo word that means 'Go this way.' Well, my buddy transmitted a similar word for them and he was answered by a babble of voices. Actually what he did was to direct fire aimlessly on a perfectly free area."

Another relates that he and the men working with him on Okinawa were often annoyed when the Japanese would blow horns into the mike (after finding their frequencies), beat tin cans and yell. He continues:

I'd say, "Don't mind those sons of bitches; tell them to go to hell and take the following message. The message begins *here*. This is to *all units*. It has *priority number one*. Not five minutes from now, but *now* I want to get a roger from each unit. *Now!*" I might have been thought of as a slave driver. But when you're out there, you may have to go against your own personality sometimes to get things done. The men were able to sort the messages out of all those sounds made by the Japs. I heard them cussing. There are no real cuss words in Navajo; the closest is the Navajo word for *devil* or *land of the devil*. We will say, "You go the way of the cursed to the land of the devil with no return!" [the Navajo equivalent to the Anglo's "Go to hell!"].

When the First Division regrouped after casualties had been replaced, some of the code talkers joined them at Melbourne, Australia. Their first combat area was Cape Gloucester, New Guinea. On the way the buzzer sounded, "Now hear this! Now hear this!" What the men on board heard was the voice of the commander of Marine Forces in the South

Pacific, Admiral Nimitz, on tape: "The eyes and ears of the world are on you, on what you do; and the success of this operation depends on you men. Good luck and God bless you!"

This was at about four o'clock in the morning. Marines were making ready to hit the shore. The officers told them, "Those who want to see the chaplain may go at this time." Many of them went. Some went to mass—the last mass they would ever attend. Some of the men knelt before the chaplain and (in the words of a Navajo who was there) started praying, "Heavenly Father, if my turn is up and that bullet has my name on it, please I don't want it any place but between my eyes where it won't hurt. Make it quick. Call me home. Repossess me." They wept, unashamed.

The Navajo continued, "I always felt that there must have been something mysterious that told the men when their time had come. I've heard those prayers from men who never reached the beach. Some never fired a shot after their prayer; some never even saw the enemy. Some of them were like the boys I saw at Peleliu . . . dead and their bodies floating on the tide to the shore, face down. That's the way it was."

There was one person who knew at all times where the First Division was: Tokyo Rose.[6] According to the author's informer, this is what she said that morning over the radio before the men hit the beach: "We know where you are . . . about to try to take Gloucester. But back home the 4-F's are lying easy and having a good time with your sweethearts . . . your loved ones that you left at home. People are having a great time in the city of Los Angeles, Denver, Kansas City, *your* city. They're praying and they're hoping and they're saying, 'Please, God, let this war go on four more years at least. We're getting rich; we're making good money; we're

6. Tokyo Rose was a graduate of the University of California at Los Angeles, an American girl of Japanese descent, who was visiting in Japan when the war broke out. She first called herself *Ann* (short for *Announcer*), and then "*Orphan Annie, your favorite enemy.*" The Americans nicknamed her *Tokyo Rose.*

having such a good time.' Your very sweethearts that you trust —your wives—they're in bed in the state of Utah, Arizona, Ohio, Texas, Pennsylvania. Think about that, First Marine. Think about that. You're about to hit the beach. Think about that!''

The Marines went ashore at Cape Gloucester just at daylight. It was the monsoon season and there was a slow drizzling rain. Some of the best code talkers were lost here— partly due to the fact that they were used as runners most of the time—a hazardous assignment.

On Peleliu, code talkers were also often used for regular Marine duty rather than as communicators. They were machine-gunners—B.A.R. men lugging Brownie Automatic rifles, infantrymen, stretcher-bearers, pressed into these duties because there weren't enough men to do these jobs. After all, there were about two thousand casualties in a period of two hours on Peleliu. One Navajo says, "I was supposed to be a signal man—the chief of the message center, but when the call came for me to do all these other things I obeyed orders. You did just what your commander told you to do, with no questions asked!"

It is said the Third Amphibious Corps reported that the use of Navajos during the Guam and Peleliu operations "was considered indispensable for the rapid transmission of classified dispatches. Enciphering and deciphering time would have prevented vital operational information from being dispatched or delivered to staff sections with any degree of speed."

Like other Marines, many of the code talkers tell of hair-raising experiences. One, who to this day is still having to adjust to an injury suffered when "one of the big ones" exploded close by, tells what happened on one occasion:

About sundown [off Saipan] I was told to make a call to shore. The first wave had hit the shore when I radioed, "How is it on the island?" The answer was "Pretty rough. They're being killed all around." That evening when I went in, our boat turned over before we landed, about 300 yards from the beach. I was almost drowned. I took off my pack, but somehow it got caught on something—maybe it was my gas mask that I hadn't taken off. So I was dragging that pack. As I was coming ashore someone cut off the pack with a combat knife, and dragged me up on shore. Water was coming out of my mouth and nose; but I survived, and we found our company that night.

The next morning another guy (white) and I went down to shore to get that pack. We saw a lot of Marines that had been killed, still on the beach. We took our choice of packs and rifles. About that time a tank landed and we followed it, which we found wasn't too bright an idea. The Japs zeroed in on that tank and started throwing mortar shells on it. A shell exploded right near me. I felt funny all over—my head felt enormous! It was like that for a week.

Tragedy and comedy walk hand in hand in dramatic situations, such as the one graphically related by the code talker who found it necessary to leave the communications school, because of having gone AWOL (mentioned in chapter three):

My reconnaissance outfit went to Iwo Jima three days before the initial attack. I was with headquarters so was back about five miles. Some boys went all the way 'round the island, scouting to decide where the invasion should take place. Twelve out of the fifty never came back.

When we went in, the top commander said, "Since you guys did the dangerous scouting, you will be on the third wave, instead of the first." Well, the first wave couldn't make it. The call went out for them to turn back. They were being hit right and left. They didn't have a chance. The men backed up and bombers were called for . . . and came. The second wave was called in when the bombers had gone, but the same thing happened. I decided right then and there I was going to tell my coxswain to zig zag. All the others had gone straight in. Our lieutenant (the one we called Stormy) said, "Corporal, I want you to get in the bow of the Higgins boat where the gate goes down." (That's the prize seat!) I got those men sitting down, and every once in a while the enemy would shoot over us. I was scared. Those fellows were kneeling down, and every once in a while one would say, "Chief, aren't you scared?" I'd say, "No, I'm not scared." I guess I didn't show it, but inside I was really scared.

The third night, just as we finally got across the airfield there, the Japanese were 'way up high on a hill and they were really shooting at us. When we got to the foot of the hill, we found a little knoll that we wanted to cross that night. And so it was planned: "Tonight at midnight, when they start shooting that first flare, everybody look straight ahead, because we are going to advance two hundred yards." We didn't know there was a graveyard over that knoll—with tombstones, four, five, six feet high.

Three of us were together. There were three other Navajos 'way up at the other end of the line. When that first flare went up we started moving. We had sticks and a piece of pipe to check for traps in front of us. We kept going. We timed ourselves. In 15 minutes or so we stopped and dug in. We found the place was all cinders so it was not difficult to dig a place to sit down in a hurry.

Well, here we were sitting in that hole with just our heads above ground when it was time for another flare. (They shoot them over the enemy lines, you know.) That second flare started wavering, and I suppose it was the shadow of those tombstones that we took for Japs coming right at us. They looked as if they were moving! So we started shooting, and we heard our own men yell, "Hey . . . you'll give away our position!" Boy, we quit in a hurry when we saw we were shooting at tombstones. Then we saw we had dug a hole in a grave. Now you know, Navajos aren't real happy in such a situation, but we couldn't do anything about it.

I hadn't slept for three days, but I didn't think I could sleep, so I told one of the guys to take his turn and the two of us would watch. He insisted that I sleep while he watched, but he was finally elected. He finally snuggled down, removed his helmet, and settled for a nice nap. Then he started yelling. We wondered what in the world was the matter. We said, "What's wrong? What's wrong?" He was yelling, "Help! Help!" We couldn't see anything and we wondered if he had jumped out and got caught.

Then the flare came again and we could see him. A sand crab (a big fellow) lay right across his neck with his pincers around his throat. Since we Indians don't like graves and dead people, this made it all scarier than ever. We were glad when daylight came. There was no sleeping for any of us that night!

It is said that in almost every operation during the war—through the Solomons, in the Marianas, at Peleliu and Iwo Jima, G-2 answered dozens of false calls to listen in on what sounded like Japanese dialect. En route to Iwo Jima, according to an article in *The Leatherneck*, "Aboard the Fifth Division's command ship, a navy commodore mistook the code talk of two Navajos for Japanese. The communicators had set up with division headquarters on deck and the navy officer was on the bridge." The author of the article says that the officer shouted into his set, "Cut that interference!" The Navajos continued dispatching without a break. "If you don't cut out that x?!--! interference, I'll come in there myself and get you guys!" he yelled. The Fifth's signal officer "never told the navy commodore that the strange tongue which gurgled in his earphones was Navajo."[7]

Richard F. Newcomb in his book, *Iwo Jima*, in discussing the preparation for the invasion of that island says, "Infantrymen cleaned their weapons, recleaned them, packed and repacked ammunition, sharpened their knives and bayonets. Drivers checked their vehicles and communications men tried out their equipment. In the USS *Cecil*, the Navajo teams had a final run-through. In a test over a circuit running from General Rockey's headquarters topside to a compartment below decks, four Indians beat four Anglo Marines in speed and accuracy of message transmission."[8]

One talker reports that he and his cousin worked as a team

7. Vernon Langille, "Indian War Call," *The Leatherneck*, vol. 31-A, March, 1948, p. 37.
8. Richard F. Newcomb, *Iwo Jima*, San Francisco: Holt, Rinehart and Winston, 1965, pp. 65, 66.

during the invasion of Iwo Jima. As he remembers, there were about twenty-five code talkers in his division (the Fourth). The division was detailed to take the airport: the Fifth Division was to take Mount Suribachi. The Third Division was standing by in case they would be needed. There were code talkers in the Fifth Division and at communications headquarters on board ship. Messages were sent in Navajo from division to division, and from ship to shore, regulating mortar fire. He remembers one message particularly that he received from his cousin stationed on the ship, telling the front lines to move back so that they could fire into the area.

The same Navajo relates a little incident on Iwo Jima as the men neared Mount Suribachi. "I heard a little noise up there . . . some small crackling sounds and a voice pleading, 'Mizu . . . Mizu.' Well, then there was a machine gun—a tracer. Then a shell from the ship, bursting all over. Then everything was quiet. I guess the man was dying. After I went to Japan with the occupation forces, I learned the Japanese language and found that the man had been saying, 'Water . . . water!' "

Major Howard M. Conner, in commenting on the gallantry of the code talkers, said, "Were it not for the Navajos, the Marines would never have taken Iwo Jima!" This is his version of the capture of that strategic area:

The entire operation was directed by Navajo code. Our corps command post was on a battleship from which orders went to the three division command posts on the beachhead, and on down to the lower echelons. I was signal officer of the Fifth Division. During the first forty-eight hours, while we were landing and consolidating our shore positions, I had six Navajo radio nets operating around the clock. In that period alone they sent and received over eight hundred messages without an error.

Weeks later, when our flag was raised over Mount Suribachi, word of that event came in the Navajo code. The commanding general was amazed. How, he wanted to know, could a Japanese name be sent in the Navajo language?

73

Iwo Jima (*USMC*)

The Navajo who sent the message had probably pronounced that Japanese word, *Sheep-uncle-ram-ice-bear-ant-cat-horse-itch*, or he might have used the nickname that one talker and his teammate used, *Mount Seppa.*

As has already been noted, it was necessary for the code talkers to adopt new words in the field. They actually had a revision, unwritten, because weapons had been developed since the formation of the original code, as well as new methods in which they were employed. There were new types of planes flown by the United States Armed Forces, and by 1943, new types of craft were afloat. The men had to come up with words for such weapons as *bazooka*, and words for ways of employing aerial attacks such as *strafing*. They had to assign a word to the device used by the Marines through which one could see human beings in the black of night.

By the end of the war, 450 men had been recruited for the Navajo communication school. Only 30 failed to qualify for service as code talkers with the Marine Corps in the Central and South Pacific. Mr. Johnston recalls one very able Navajo who was dropped because he just could not resist overindulging in "firewater." Shore patrol picked him up repeatedly and put him in the brig. When he muffed that "last chance" he was let out of the program and sent overseas.

Sergeant Johnston stayed with the program at Camp Pendleton until August, 1944, and was discharged from the service about a month later. He had one regret—he had been retained at home base, and had not been given the assignment of overseas training of the talkers in Hawaii!

Chapter Seven

A PROFILE OF EXPERIENCES IN THE PACIFIC

... We made history!

Life was difficult (at best) on the islands. The grass grew to a height of four or five feet, concealing booby traps and skulking enemies while generally impeding progress. There were mosquitoes and other insects, snipers, thirst, malaria and gastroenteritis. One writer reports that memory of the simplest creature comforts such as warm water and a bed with clean sheets, existed only in dreams for the man in the jungle.

Charles Newman reports in the Fourth Marine Division Association newsletter of March, 1973, that a medical officer attached to one battalion of the Fourth Division is supposed to have given the following medical bulletin before their assault on Saipan:

> In the surf, beware of sharks, barracuda, sea snakes, anemones, razor sharp coral, polluted water, poison fish and giant clams that shut on a man like a bear trap— ashore, there is leprosy, typhus, filariasis, yaws, typhoid, dengue fever, dysentery, saber grass, insects, snakes and giant lizards. Eat nothing growing on the islands, don't drink its water and don't approach the inhabitants.

John Toland, historian, describes Guadalcanal in this way:

> From the air Guadalcanal looked like a tropical paradise of lush green mountains, forested shores and colorful coral reefs. In reality it was paradise lost, a study in dramatic contrasts—peaks, barren hills and dense dark green jungles,

76

Two Indian Marine observers on hill overlooking Garapan, a city on the island of Saipan, Marianas. (*USMC*)

Indian communicators at work in Bougainville jungles. (*USMC*)

white cockatoos and ferocious white ants, myna birds and malarial mosquitoes, bone chilling torrential rains and insufferably hot dusty plains. It was an island of bananas, limes, papayas—and crocodiles, giant lizards, fungus infections, poisonous spiders, leeches and scorpions.[9]

The Indians seemed to be better prepared to cope with the situation than most of the Anglos. Ruth Underhill, in her book entitled *Here Come the Navajo*, writes: "These young men had never fought before, but they had some of the skill possessed by their fighting ancestors." She says that they could crawl through the jungle without a sound, taking cover behind bushes their white comrades had hardly noticed. The manner in which they could get around at night amazed the other Marines. They were accustomed to desert darkness, instead of lighted streets. She writes, "The fighting, especially in the jungle, was much on the old Indian style. This meant sudden attacks by a small group of men, rushing from cover. It meant tracking single enemies through the jungle and watching the chance for a quick deadly spring."[10]

An article in *Headquarters Bulletin*, September, 1944, carried a story in which Sergeant Frank Few, Indian Marine, is reported to have amazed everyone by his display of stamina:

Sgt. Frank Few was one of three Marines who returned from an ill-fated expedition which was ambushed by the Japs. Attacked by an enemy soldier, his machine gun jammed and he was struck in the arm and chest with a bayonet. But he knocked the Jap's rifle away, choked him and then stabbed him with the Jap's own bayonet. He borrowed a fellow Marine's pistol to kill another Jap and then succeeded in getting his own gun working by putting a cartridge in the chamber each time he fired. Using this method he killed one more of the Nipponese force before he again joined the main body of Marines to battle with them

9. John Toland, *The Rising Sun*, New York: Random House, 1970, p. 348.
10. Ruth Underhill, *Here Come the Navajo*, Department of the Interior, New York: Haskell Press, 1953, p. 255.

against the attacking unit. When the Leathernecks' chances appeared hopeless, Few and two other survivors finally dashed for the water. He swam four and a half miles through shark-infested waters before reaching safety. And at the end of the ordeal, those who interviewed him said he hardly seemed physically tired.[11]

Another writer says of the Indians, that their racial characteristics—stoicism, keen sense of perception enabling them to spot a snake by sound or smell, long sleek muscles built for almost indefatigable endurance, extraordinary muscular coordination, and an almost weird faculty for crossing any kind of terrain in the dark—made them indispensable warriors.

Through the years the Navajos have demonstrated their fear of dead bodies, a fact that was of some concern to Marine officers.

One Navajo reports that his mother, who died when he was six years old, was buried on a neighboring hill—not far from the hogan. He was forbidden to visit the grave because his elders believed her spirit might come to him in the night to strangle him. One day, a few years after his mother's death, he unthinkingly wandered to the spot where his mother lay, stumbling over the grave. He was terrified. But days passed and nothing happened. He has realized for many years, of course, that the superstition has no basis.

As far back as 1902, we have an example of this fear of a dead body. During that year the federal government appropriated the sum of $500 to build a dam and irrigation system on the reservation. One of the Navajos died while digging a ditch on the project, and the white men buried him. The next day, word got around that the shovel used to dig the grave was in the hands of a certain Navajo workman on the job. When the man discovered the offending object in his hands, he dropped it and vigorously rubbed sand on his hands to rid them of the *chendi* (evil spirit).

However, when the Navajos went into the combat area, the

11. "Red Man Hits the War Path," *Headquarters Bulletin,* September, 1944, p. 19.

sight of dead bodies seemed to bother them not at all. They accepted their presence as a part of the whole situation. One code talker says that they used to cover the dead wherever they lay. They rarely had a hot meal, but sat on a stump and had something to eat from their mess kits; there would be dead bodies all around at times. They just had to live with it and paid no more attention to the enemy dead than did the white Marines in the outfit.

Navajos (like Anglos) differed in their reaction to stress in combat. One says, "The only thing that bothered me was the big shells and bombs. When they landed close by and shook the whole ground, it was no wonder that some of the men went cuckoo. Small fire didn't bother me at all."

Another reports that he was "all curiosity" at first and quick to shoot; during his second campaign he was more hesitant, more careful; during the third (which was on Peleliu) he struggled with himself for control, but "went through with it," obeying all commands; during the fourth (on Okinawa) life didn't mean much to him anymore. He became resigned to death—almost immune to feeling. He adds, "It is very sad when you don't care for *yourself* anymore."

An ex-Marine Navajo (not a communicator) relates a mystical experience that is perhaps puzzling to some, but in its way very beautiful. One night, huddled in a New Guinea foxhole, under orders not to leave it under any circumstances because the enemy surrounded the area, he was trying to sleep. He did not know until later that at that very moment, his sister and grandmother (with the medicine man, relatives and friends) were conducting a ceremony over his civilian clothes, asking the Spirit to protect him and return him to them safely. He says that at last he fell into a sort of trance—like a dream— and he heard the medicine man singing.

During a ceremony such as this (he says) it is the tradition for the one being blessed to stretch out his arms, and using a sort of "gathering-in" motion, bring the fresh pure air into his "heart"—four times, to make him strong. Quietly leaving his foxhole in the tropical night, this Navajo reports,

I walked through the jungle and it was filled with light—like in early morning. I walked through the trees, brought the pure night air into my heart, and presented myself to God that I might be a perfect man, that I might be strong against the enemy, and that I should be returned to my people. Then I came back to the foxhole and woke up. But it had not been a dream—I had really walked, for I saw my tracks in the soft ground. After that I had no fears. I was *never* afraid again!

Later when the enemy bombed us as we hit the beach on Leyte Island (Philippines) and everything was "red, blue and black together," my white friend and I knew we would be safe. We fell between planks that had been unloaded from the boat, and lay there as the tracers came down—just like rain. When the raid was over and we got up and looked around us at the men who had been killed by bombs and wounded by shrapnel, we found that, even though the planks had been literally chewed by shrapnel, neither of us had gotten even a scratch. I knew then that the ceremony my family had had with the medicine man singing had protected me from all danger. I came out of the war without being touched by the enemy.

One communicator confesses that he never sent a message without first asking the Spirit to help him. It is quite possible that many of the others followed this practice.

Marine authorities were confident that the Japanese would not be able to break the code; however, as a protective measure, great care was taken to keep the program secret. In the combat areas, security agents kept a wary eye on broadcast circuits, looking for scripts that might have been carelessly left in view and that might be helpful to the enemy should the stations be captured. On one occasion they found an Arizona trade journal carrying an article about life on the Navajo reservation. The agents seized the magazine with some apprehension, but they were able to breathe freely after perusing the article, finding it harmless.

Navajo instructors of code talkers drilled into the men the deep necessity for "devotion to the cause." One of them says,

I wanted those code talkers to guard their secrets with their lives. I thought of the idea of comparing them with the Japanese suicide pilots and the Nazi elite guards. If they were captured, they should guard the code with their lives! I would ask, "Would you refuse to give away the secret of the code if you had a samurai sword at your throat? If the enemy would ask, 'What is your word for *A*?' would you tell them? You begin to bleed; you begin to feel your own blood trickling down . . . warm, with the cutting a little deeper. You *would* lay down your life before you would tell, wouldn't you?"

I would look them square in the eye and ask them to answer *yes* or *no*. I would say, "Are you devoted that much? Are you willing to die for this secret method?"

As an instructor in the field I ramrodded that. If, when I asked a question, a man would nod his head, I would say, "No . . . I don't see a thing in your eye. If you say 'Uh-huh' I don't understand you. Say 'Yes, sir!' " If it wasn't definite enough to suit me I would say, "I didn't quite hear you!" He'd say it a little louder but I would answer him again, "I don't quite hear you!" Then he'd say with emphasis, "Yes, sir!" I'd stay with it until I heard it loud and clear, and then I knew that I could trust that man—just like the suicide pilots would give their lives when they made that last dive. They would say, "More blood for the Emperor." Like the Nazi Elite Corps—no *if* or *maybe* about the way they did things. I wanted absolutely strict discipline—military discipline.

After serving as a code talker for a while, one of the men changed over to radio repair. Of course, if messages came through in Navajo, he would try to get them. He always had work to do on the equipment. When he had completed repair on a radio he would take it back to the front lines, or wherever he had gotten it, pick up equipment that needed checking over and return with it.

One day in Wellington, New Zealand, as he was checking out a set, he dialed in on some Navajos talking from Auckland. He changed to transmitting frequencies and tried to

Pfc. Preston Toledo and Pfc. Frank Toledo (*USMC*)

break in to "give the guys a bum message." He tried every possible way to "throw them off" but they remained unperturbed by the intrusion. He was on the line four or five minutes, but he could not get the men to divulge the division or company they were with. As he says, "They just wouldn't buy it." He wrote down their message, but couldn't decipher it. He says that after the retraining sessions in Hawaii, some of the original terms were changed, along with the addition of new terms, which made his decoding of their message impossible. That experience demonstrated to him that the boys were "really with it."

Concern that the dark-complexioned Navajos might be mistaken for Japanese was well founded.

In the latter days of Guadalcanal, an army unit picked up a Navajo code talker on the coastal road and sent the message to the Marine command: "We have captured a Jap in Marine clothing with Marine identification tags." When an officer confronted the captive, he immediately released him as an Indian communicator, who (it is said) was "bored with the proceedings."

The situation did not always prove to be "boring." One Navajo tells of his experiences concerning incidents on New Georgia Island:

> After we had hiked two or three days, right at dusk in the jungle, the Japs hit our line. When we were under fire, one army officer pulled his .45 pistol on me, taking me for a Jap. You see, my beard grows like a Jap's—straight down. An Anglo beard will follow the contour of the chin. So I had a hard time convincing that officer that I was an American Marine. They threatened to shoot me, but took me to headquarters at my insistence, where I was identified. I couldn't shave out there in the jungle, and so I was actually captured twice because of my beard. Most of the Indian boys had very little beard, but *I* did—'way down there.

Another hair-raising experience is related by another code talker:

Corporal Lloyd Oliver of Ship Rock, New Mexico, operating a field radio with a Marine artillery regiment in the South Pacific. (*USMC*)

I had been on Guadalcanal for some time and was hungry for something like orange juice. The army usually had some, and a transport had just come in close to where we were waiting on the beach to leave the island. I walked over to the army supplies and started digging for orange juice when somebody put an iron in my back. I thought whoever it was was just kidding and kept on digging. He finally said, "Get out of there, you damn Jap!" The sergeant standing there said, "He has Marine Corps identification and speaks good English." The man with the gun said, "I don't care if he graduated from Ohio State. We're going to shoot him."

I finally mumbled, "I'm from right down there," but I couldn't see the direction because there was too much sweat running down into my eyes. Finally, they took me back to my outfit. I had 15 men around me, and the sergeant of the guard had a .45 cocked against my back all the way and I had my hands up all the way. When we got to the beach, they asked, "Is this your man?" and of course got the answer, "Yeah . . . that's our man. Hey—are you guys serious?" "You're damn right we're serious," they said. "If you guys don't make a positive identification we're going to take him back."

Finally the lieutenant came around and said, "What's the matter?" "Well, we caught this man over there in our yard and we think he's a Jap. If you don't identify him we're going to take him back over there and shoot him."

After that they gave me a bodyguard. If I went to the head, he would come along behind me (this tall white man); I'd go swimming and he'd go swimming. They made him stick right by me. One night we had a bombing attack . . . and I was there all by myself. Everybody (including my bodyguard) had taken off for the hills, but I was stuck there.

Louis Steinbacher recalls another case of mistaken identity among the Navajos. The Fourth Division had landed on the south beaches of Saipan and the Second Marine Division had landed abreast on the left. The 27th Army Division was floating reserve. A few days after D-Day, when the jeep radios

Indians with the Marines on Saipan. (*USMC*)

Indians make good scouts. (*USMC*)

came in, he was in communication with another corporal of the company. Mr. Steinbacher was in one division sector with a Navajo and the other was with a Navajo over in the Second Division. The two men were working as liaison between the two divisions. It was shortly after they were set up, on one occasion, when Mr. Steinbacher failed to "raise" the corporal on his radio. He tried repeatedly, and finally notified message center. They evidently got word by telephone or runner to the Second Division and cleared up the situation. This was the story: Evidently men of the Second Marine Division (at least one particular group of the division) were not aware that Indians were among them. The corporal had left the Navajo in charge of the radio jeep while he was scrounging up some food or what-have-you. Along came some Marines and saw the Navajo in the jeep. Thinking he was a Japanese, they grabbed him, even though he tried to explain his identify as a Marine. It just didn't "go over" with his captors.

"So you're an American with the Fourth Marine Division, eh? O.K. . . . who is the Commandant of the Marine Corps?" The answer should have been, "General Vandergrift," but the Navajo, misinterpreting the question, gave the name of his commanding officer, Captain Watson. With this, they tossed him behind barbed wire. When the corporal returned he had some explaining to do before the Navajo was released.

One code talker had been shocked by a mortar shell that exploded close to his ear; he had the uncomfortable sensation that his head was of mammoth size. One day he found a shell hole with a lot of water in it, so he decided to take a bath (along with other members of his company), thinking that if he washed all over, putting a lot of water on his head, that miserable sensation might be minimized. He removed his clothes and bathed, taking his time, and did not notice that all the others had finished and had left him alone.

When the Japanese were taken prisoner, they were usually requested to strip to uncover any hidden weapons. An M.P. who seemed to appear out of nowhere probably took the bather for a Japanese prisoner. He yelled, "Get out!" The

Pfc. Cecil G. Trosip Oraibi, Arizona, at communication system on Saipan. (*USMC*)

Indian Marine Fighters on Bougainville. (*USMC*)

Navajo turned around and confronted the M.P. who placed his bayonet right between the eyes of the startled Indian, who said, "I'm one of the Marines!" About that time one of his buddies appeared and said, "Yeah . . . this is one of our men!" He was allowed to put his clothes on, but the M.P. didn't leave his post. He turned the Navajo in to the commanding officer who made positive identification. It was a close call.

The same code talker reports that during an advance, when they were flushing the enemy out of shell holes with hand grenades, they took a lot of prisoners. One day the commander called, "Geronimo! Come here! Take these prisoners back to the C.P. where the other men are. Make the prisoners keep their hands up all the way; and if they try any funny business, shoot!" When the Navajo arrived back at platoon headquarters, everybody started laughing. They said, "Which is the prisoner? Which are the Japanese?"

Another incident (or rather the danger of it) concerns a group of Navajos who one day worked with the communication section, stringing telephone wires a considerable distance ahead of the C.P., well into the area. All were supposed to be back during daylight, but they were delayed so much that it was more dark than daylight when they returned. There was some sort of parapet for them to come over, and just inside, a guard stood with a .45 pointed right at the place a man's head would first appear. Everything was fine until one of the Indians stuck his head up and nearly lost it when the guard mistook him for a Japanese.

Colonel James Tinsley says, "We had to watch the war dogs carefully when they were around the Navajos—they couldn't tell them from Japs."

It was discovered after the war that some of the Japanese were confused on seeing the Navajos and conjectured that they were natives of Alaska.

The Navajos were resourceful. Here is one example.

For some reason, on Okinawa, there was a shortage of

supplies for the Marines, although the army did not suffer. One of the code talkers describes the situation and tells how they met it:

We were ill-fed. So we gathered up all the rifles that we could find, all the Japanese flags we could find, all the weapons that the Japanese had abandoned, along with field officers' boots, and traded them for food from the doggies (this is what we called the army men). We knew that the sugar, meat and sometimes fruit were with the forward echelon of the army. So we traded souvenirs for food.

Some of us Indians would sneak around in the ravines and maybe see a stray goat; we'd skin it, build a fire and cook it. We'd kill a horse, butcher it and roast it. Our commanding officer would admit that the chow was low and suggested that we might trade captured ammunition or any of the other souvenirs named, with that army unit. We actually loaded a jeep and hauled the stuff over there in broad daylight. We were caught by battalion commanders one day and they emphatically told us that we *couldn't do that!*

One day we spotted a young colt. We shot it and crawled over in the ravine, skinned it out, and we heard our white brothers say, "Hey ... they've got some meat over there." So we invited them to join us. It was in the afternoon. We built a fire, and while the fire was going we saw spotter planes coming over; but you can be sure there was no one around that fire when the planes strafed that spot. After they had gone we put the meat on the hot coals.

Those white guys said, "Hey, Chief, where did you get this meat?" They thought we had traded souvenirs for this good beef. "Over there ... over the hill!" I said vaguely.

Finally, after they had salted the meat and eaten it, smacked their lips over it, one of the guys who knew what it was, pointed to the skin over in the ravine and said, "Hey, Chief ... pretty good horse!" And turning to our guests, said, "Don't you know that you just got through filling up with horse meat?" Surprisingly, they didn't seem to mind, and echoed, "Sure, Chief ... pretty good horse!"

Pfc. Samuel Sandoval, a radio operator from Farmington, New Mexico, relaxes under the Tori Gate, surveying the scenic beauties of Okinawa shrine. (*USMC*)

The Navajo's sense of humor is reflected frequently in "war stories" as related by both Anglos and the code talkers themselves (noted frequently in the foregoing pages). Ernie Pyle, in one of his latest dispatches from Okinawa, described a ceremonial dance put on by the First Division's Navajos before leaving for Okinawa. In this ceremony, they prayed to the gods to sap the strength of the Japanese as they stormed the beaches. Anglo Marines watched with interest and amusement, but the Indians did not fail to point out later the ease with which the landing had been made, and reminded the Anglos of their ceremony.

When the First Division met strong opposition in the south of Okinawa, later, one white Marine said to a Navajo, "O.K., what about your little ceremony? What do you call this?" The Navajo smiled and answered, "This is different. We prayed only for an easy landing."

One Marine officer recalls that there was something humorous about the way the code talkers worked. He says:

As you know, messages begin and end with naval time: e.g., 0900 plus days with one to nine using 101900, etc., thus using a lot of 0's. Hearing the Navajo word for zero (nos-bas) was the only way we could tell when the message being sent was near the end. (This was the only word I knew in Navajo.) We used to say to the Navajo, "Come on, Chief, you're saying a lot more than is in the message. You're shooting the breeze with your Navajo buddy." He would invariably answer, "No stein."

The Navajos responded to the nickname, *Chief*, repeatedly and in some cases to *Geronimo*, as has already been noted.

The Navajos are a proud people. One example is cited by Joseph W. Creagh, who served along with the Indians in the teletype service of the Signal Company, Headquarters Battalion. He says that while on the island of Tinian they began to receive ten-in-one rations. Since there were five men in the teletype section and five Navajo code talkers at headquarters, the ten-in-one rations were issued to the teletype section with

Marine Indian uses walky-talky. (*USMC*)

Private Leslie Hemstreet of Crystal, New Mexico, beats native drum at a shrine on Okinawa. (*USMC*)

instructions to share with the Indians. The Navajos would not eat with the teletype section. Mr. Creagh had an idea as to the reason and the second day he arranged for the ten-in-one rations to be issued to the Navajos with instructions to share with the teletype section. The plan worked very well.

T. O. Kelly, CWO, USMC, Ret., describes the way in which some of the Navajos celebrated final victory:

> The Navajos' innate imperturbability was thoroughly and completely shattered when early one night in August, 1945, news came over the division radio net that Emperor Hirohito had asked for "peace terms." Naturally the Navajos were the first to learn this good news. The overjoyed Navajos decided that a celebration was in order. As tom-toms were not items of issue, they headed *au naturel* for the bandsmen's tents. Grabbing drums, and later any instruments available, they Indian-danced their way toward the officers' tent country. The bandsmen, also *au naturel* were in hot pursuit, trying to retrieve their drums.[12]

Joseph Creagh comments that after the Japanese surrender, the men were ordered to participate in some athletic event every day. The Navajos faithfully obeyed orders, going out every morning and afternoon to play softball. Sometimes some of the others would drift off into the woods and relax, playing cards or reading; but they would march back to the area double time so they would be sweaty and grimy on arrival.

Satisfaction with the performance of the code talkers in their sensitive assignment was expressed many, many times by officers who used them for sending operational orders, and by other Marines who worked along with them. High-ranking military men questioned at first whether or not the Navajo communicators could be relied upon for accuracy. Hazards to be faced should errors in transmission or translation be made were almost unthinkable. One can scarcely imagine the

12. T. O. Kelly, "Navajo Talkers Confused the Japanese . . . and Sometimes the Marines," *From Our Heritage*, July, 1971, p. 28.

Indian communicators at work in Bougainville jungles. (*USMC*)

tragedy of a battalion commander in the position of trying to explain a gigantic loss of men because his Indian code talker had told him the order was to attack instead of withdraw. However, the Indians came through with incredible accuracy and infallible dependability.

Colonel William N. McGill (Ret.), reports that he listened to a couple of Navajos working one time and found it very amusing ... and confounding. It was astounding that the message grunted at one end of the wire came out the same at the other end.

Lieutenant Colonel J. B. Berkeley, a communications officer with the Fifth Amphibious Corps, says it was demonstrated time and again when these teams were given complicated reports and instructions to transmit by voice over radio or wire that not a single mistake was made, a fact the regular communications men speaking in code could not match.

Colonel Marlowe C. Williams, USMC (Ret.) (who served as commanding officer on Bougainville, Guam and Iwo Jima), says of the Navajos: "In my opinion, these talkers were invaluable throughout the assault on Guam and other campaigns prior and subsequent to this one."

Lieutenant General R. E. Cushman, Jr., testifies, "The Navajo code talkers, of course, prevented the enemy from understanding the messages and, therefore, were of considerable value."

When asked the question, "How would you personally evaluate the contribution of the code talkers in winning the ultimate victory in the Pacific?" the Navajos are modest in claiming credit for their efforts.

One says (and rightly so), "Of course it was the teamwork— a combination of all forces—that eventually won the victory. The code talkers were not used as much at first as they were later. In fact, not until the Fourth Division were they used in the way it was originally planned. After that, I think *we made history.*"

Another agrees, saying that as time went on, the talkers

became more and more important, adding, "On Iwo Jima, I could not go anywhere by myself. By command of the general, I was always to have a guard with me to protect me." (As has been noted, others had the same experience.)

A third reports: "As you know, men in the first wave on the beach during an invasion barely have a chance to survive; the second wave has a little better chance, and chances are fair for the men in the third wave. On Tarawa, they put me in the third wave to give me a better chance for survival. I was in the front lines a lot, but they would keep us where the action was only a half day—not longer than a full day—then send us back, keeping us involved, but trying to protect us in that they didn't want anything to happen to us. We couldn't be replaced like some of the men with general skills."

On September 18, 1945, the *San Diego Union* carried an article that summed up the overall picture:

> A lion's share of the credit for finding the military jack-pot since man first rose and took umbrage against his fellow man belongs to the Marine Corps. The hard-hitting leather-necks needed an unbreakable code and got it. For three years, wherever the Marines landed, the Japanese got an earful of strange gurgling noises interspersed with other sounds resembling the call of a Tibetan monk and the sound of a hot water bottle being emptied.
>
> Huddled over their radio sets in bobbing assault barges, in foxholes on the beach, in slit trenches, deep in the jungle, the Navajo Marines transmitted and received messages, orders, vital information. The Japanese ground their teeth and committed hari-kari.

In answer to the question as to whether or not he thought the Japanese sent recordings of coded messages to head-quarters in Tokyo for study during the war, Colonel Norman Gertz, who served as radio platoon commander of the Fourth Signal Company, said, "My guess is that while the Japanese may have monitored their transmissions at one time or another, that because the Navajos were used during periods of tactical engagement, the Japanese really did not have either the time or facilities to identify the transmissions properly. Having had personal observation of the Japanese electronic equipment through the Iwo Jima campaign, I can almost speculate that in the field, they did not have enough equipment to monitor our channels and record the transmissions for analysis."

On unquestioned authority the author has the information that Lieutenant General Seizo Arisue, chief of intelligence for Japan during World War II, has ruefully admitted that they were able to decipher the code system used by the American Air Force, but were unable to break the code used by the Marines. An informant told the general (in 1972) that the ingenious code was based on the language of the Navajo Indian tribe—a fact that may have served to lessen his feeling of chagrin that his cryptographers had failed in their efforts to master it.

The Marines have always been justly proud of their strategy in carrying out amphibious operations, boasting a combination of those elements necessary for success: reconnaissance, leadership, careful planning, coordination and training. During World War II, the Navajos added still another element: a system of communication that completely confused the enemy.

The contribution of the code talkers had been so invaluable that the Marine Corps wanted to keep the code as a permanent adjunct. For several months, Sergeant Johnston worked with Colonel Peterson, commander of the amphibious base at Camp Pendleton, on a plan that would be approved in Washington. However, their efforts were not successful. As Mr. Johnston now says, "Officialdom seemed to think that there would be no more wars. The code was allowed to die."

Looking back to the year 1943, we find an article that appeared in Flagstaff's *Coconino Sun* that gives tribute to the men from the reservation:

Out of the combination of the modern fighting tactics of the Marines and the inherent fighting ability of the Indians is evolving one of the hardest-hitting units of the hard-hitting Leatherneck Corps.[13]

That combination *did* evolve, hastening the termination of the conflict.

13. "Navajo Indian on Road to Tokyo," *Coconino Sun,* March 5, 1943.

Pfc. Carl Gorman of Chinle, Arizona, mans an observation post on a hill overlooking the city of Garapan. (*USMC*)

Chapter Eight
RETURN OF THE NAVAJO

. . . . It is a better world we have to build.

To write about the religion of any group of people, whether they be Irish, Nigerian, Vietnamese or Navajo, the author should tread softly. According to one definition, religion is a quest for the value of the ideal life, related to the environing universe, or recognition on the part of man of a controlling superhuman power entitled to obedience, reverence and worship. As is well known, people across the face of the earth hold to widely varying interpretations and applications of this basic premise.

Navajo religion combines a sound moral philosophy and preventive medicine. The Navajo believes that man is paramount in importance and that all the forces and glories of nature were created for his benefit. He strives to control his environment and his physical well-being by observing certain taboos and by submitting to prescribed ceremonies. His main purpose in life is to maintain harmony with nature. He is concerned only with the present life, for he believes that he will become a part of the universe after death, and having no afterlife, he expects neither to be punished nor rewarded for his way of life on earth.

The author is reminded of an article by William Hedgepath who writes of early Indians:

> They saw beasts, rocks, snakes, birds, stars, each imbued with a spirit, and a right way to be regarded in harmony with everything else.[14]

14. William Hedgepath, "Timeless People, Changing Earth," *Look* Magazine, June 2, 1970.

The Indian had a basic reason for rapport with his environment. Quoting Hedgepath again, it has been necessary, for his has been a life of

> ... tilling a surface so barren that supernatural intervention grew steadily vital to village life. As integral parts of the Creative Divinity that lives in all things they evoked all the fertile enfoldments of nature through regular ritual urgings. They sang up corn, called down rain, and dwelt together in communal harmony—dancing out their periodic prayer-dreams in exquisite seclusion upon their share of the earth's brotherly face.

Some now believe in the *yei*, the Navajo gods, but may also attend a Christian church, such as the Catholic Church. A sect called the Native American Church combines Indian tradition and Christianity. Peyote is a sacrament used by the members; rites may last all night—in a sort of group therapy session.

The Navajos express kinship with their beautiful homeland in their references to Mother Earth and Father Sky.

If a cure for a physical or emotional disturbance is called for, a medicine man performs a ritual centered on a sand painting, made of crushed red sandstone, ground charcoal, white sand and yellow ocher. The medicine man pulls the images for the painting from his mind and assistants help him execute them—geometric shapes, elongated god figures, etc. The patient then sits in the center of the painting and the medicine man touches the patient with sand scooped from the painting—to drain away the illness. (It should be noted here that some Navajos are now beginning to study medicine as it is practiced among Anglos.)

One code talker says that his mother and sister insisted that the medicine man conduct a rite preceding his departure, asking for protection for him during his term of service. Undoubtedly this type of rite was held for numerous Navajos leaving the reservation to go to war.

Most (if not all) of the Navajos took part in ceremonies

when they returned to the reservation—ceremonies designed to purify them after meeting all kinds of people on the outside, some of whom were evil, and to blot out memories of what had happened, thereby helping them to return to a normal life on the reservation.

This purification ceremony on a person's return is called the Enemy Way or Squaw Dance. It has its origin in the days when the Navajos raided the neighboring tribes or battled with the cavalry. Curative ceremonies were held after these forays.

The Enemy Way is a three-day ceremony in which the diagnostician, the herb man, and the medicine man take part. The diagnostician will tell the man what his trouble is, the herb man will prescribe herbs, and the medicine man will perform the ceremony of purification.

The medicine man has a bundle in which he places anything related to the enemy—a coat, eyeglasses, weapon—anything the Navajo may have brought back from the combat area. Some have been known to bring back skulls or parts of the enemy's bones. (Of course, in earlier days, they brought back scalps.)

The code talkers returned with bayonets, helmets, tufts of hair from Japanese victims, bits of clothing, objects taken from pockets of the enemy's uniforms, etc.

Sometimes a hole is dug, the souvenirs buried and shot at with a rifle four times, thus cutting off all bad communications between the mind of the Navajo and the enemy—feelings of guilt or regret that are causing the sickness.

Since the relatives pay for the ceremony (unless the person just returned has a great deal of money) there is a unifying influence present, with everyone involved contributing to the healing of the returnee. He is thus brought back into harmony with nature.

It is thought that an individual who does not submit to the curative ceremony may eventually suffer mentally and physically even though he does not feel the need of purification immediately on his return. The rites help to disentangle a man from his past. One of the Navajos comments, "Perhaps the army veteran who goes berserk and starts killing women and children or sniping from rooftops shooting at anyone he sees, without reason, wouldn't do this if he were relieved of the memories that made him go berserk—through submission to a ceremony like the Enemy Way."

Here is the rather poignant story concerning reliance on religion, as related to the author by a Navajo communicator:

I was 18 when I entered the service, on very short notice. I didn't even have time to go back to see my parents. All I did was write them a letter. I was working at the hospital in Fort Defiance when I suddenly made up my mind to join the Marines. I filled out my application, had my physical and was on my way. I had been exposed to the Catholic religion a little, but I admit I hadn't taken it very seriously.

I *did* pray many many times when I was exposed to danger on the main battleline, as a code talker and as a signalman. I prayed as my mother and father had taught me—to the Heavenly Being as well as to Mother Earth.

Now when I came back, surprisingly my mother told me, "Son, do you know that since you left, almost every morning, I have gone to my sacred hill and prayed, using my sacred corn pollen, that you would come back with your whole physical being and a good mind." Maybe that is the reason I came back all in one piece.

Now I did have a hell of a time with malaria; I got it on Guadalcanal. Out of about 6000 Marines over there, I was among the last 16 to get it. Some of the colonels and generals asked, "How is it with you Navajos? Are you so tough that you don't even need to take quinine?" I always said, "I don't know. I had a tough life when I was a little boy."

I came back to San Francisco, where they sent me to a rehabilitation center, then to a hospital, then home for a month's leave. I was skin and bones. I came back to Gallup where my father met me. He said, "Son, I'm glad you came back alive, I don't want you to go to town and try to have some fun; I want you to come home with me. I have something for you there." So I said, "O.K." Well, they had a medicine man there for me. They had a sing over me. My mother and father were so happy to have me back that they killed a little nine-months pet goat; it was real tender. They wanted to feed me, I was so thin. But it didn't have any taste to it. I just couldn't eat it. I had to set it aside. There was something about the malaria, the things I had gone through, the difference in the wind and air . . . well, I just couldn't eat it.

But I got well. I think my mother's prayers on her sacred hill helped me through the war and after I got back home.

The sacred corn pollen, as used by this code talker's mother, is basic in Navajo ceremonies. For instance, when a new hogan is built the medicine man conducts a *Blessingway,* during which he smears corn pollen on the poles of the hogan so that "the place will be happy." It is thought that corn is actually a sacred plant. The pollen is shaken off the tassel into a small individual pouch made of deerskin, which is blessed in a prescribed ceremony.

Certain gestures accompany the use of the pollen in prayer. A bit of the pollen is placed on the tongue to purify speech; some is then placed on the soft spot on the head to signify purification of the soul—the thought process. A little is spilled toward the east to symbolize the fact that during prayer it was being presented to the gods.

The mother of the code talker, in her ceremonial prayer on her sacred hill, attempted to close all gates necessary to hold back evil or detrimental forces that might prey upon her son, putting an invisible force around him.

When the bombs fell on Pearl Harbor in 1941, the Navajos were quietly living out their lives in their own way, secluded from the pulsating life of the twentieth century. World War II jolted them into active participation in meeting the crisis that faced the nation. The effect on the Navajo and on his way of life was far-reaching.

The hardest part for many was the shock of being rejected

for active service because they couldn't speak English. The result was a sudden demand for education. Of the 420 code talkers, 290 had been trained in federal high schools.

According to the Treaty of 1868, Navajo children from six to sixteen were to be compelled to attend school; but there had been strong resistance to this part of the agreement. Before 1946, officials of the Bureau of Indian Affairs had to round up Navajo children, practically kidnapping them, to force them to go to school. After the war, they couldn't hold back the tide. The whole educational system had to be revised to meet the demand.

One Navajo had written home from overseas, "I could be a technical sergeant, only I haven't had enough school. Make my little brother go to school even if you have to lasso him."

Most Navajo children are now able to attend school, through the twelfth grade. But for those who have somehow missed their chance for a rudimentary education, and are somewhat illiterate, a program has been set up whereby they may learn the fundamentals. One code talker is now an educator in this program, with students ranging from 19 to 81 years of age. The people come in groups to his town and other places, and learn how to sign their names (instead of signing with a thumbprint); how to read simple things like road signs (thus promoting safety on the highway); how to choose foods for a balanced diet; and how to read prices in stores, and make correct change.

Raymond Nakai, recent chairman of the Navajo nation, stated,

> From the service, the Navajo got a glimpse of what the rest of the world is doing. The Marines particularly did a great deal for him—not only in giving him a view of the outside world, but in giving him a glimmer of hope and the necessary vision of the benefits that can be derived from certain things he has seen throughout the world.

In response to the comment that World War II had revealed the need for an education (as exemplified in qualifications requisite to becoming a code talker), he agreed, but added, "The Navajo needs this type of education as a supplement to his strong basic, *informal* education, inherent in his rich traditional culture."

Through the years since the return of the Navajo from World War II, great strides have been made in both directions —toward formal as well as informal education. Public schools, as well as boarding schools established by the Bureau of Indian Affairs have multiplied in number. It is still as difficult for the little ones who enter such schools for the first time to face instruction almost completely in English, as it was for the men who marched off to war thirty years ago. But officials are striving to perfect better instructional methods in teaching English to ease the difficulties for children who from birth have heard only the Navajo tongue. Dr. Gergman, psychiatrist, told Ralph Looney, author of an article in *National Geographic,* "It's as if you or I were to be forcibly enrolled in Moscow University and expected to learn astronomy in classes taught in Russian."[15]

Determined to promulgate the skills and traditions of the tribe, the Navajos have established the tribe-controlled Rough Rock Demonstration School in an Arizona trading-post settlement, about 120 miles from Gallup, New Mexico.

Rug-weaving and other traditional arts are kept alive under experts, as well as "hogan-housekeeping." Navajo teachers give instruction in the native tongue, teaching English as a second language.

Here also are taught the intricate ceremonies of the medicine man. Each of six medicine men instructs two, working with them in the privacy of his own home.

At Rough Rock, they feel it is important that the graduate shall be comfortable in the white man's world, but that he shall also be steeped in Navajo lore and—as has been said— trained in Navajo skills.

The Navajo "mystic," referred to earlier, who heard the

15. Ralph Looney, "The Navajo Nation Looks Ahead," *National Geographic,* vol. 142, no. 6, December, 1972, p. 774.

medicine man singing in his foxhole, based his whole attitude toward life on what he learned from his grandfather:

My grandfather was a great man. He said, "Educate yourself but we will help you. We will tell you which rattlesnake has poison, and where it is safe to walk. You will get a soreness if you walk in the poison ivy. Don't walk near a cliff for a devil might push you over. Don't throw a rock at a man; don't throw a rock at a woman; don't be afraid of animals. They do not dislike you. Be spiritual. Don't play cards because you might lose your property. Know things in nature are like a person. Talk to the tornados; talk to the thunder. They are your friends and will protect you."

The average, modern, educated Navajo may not agree that a devil might push him off the cliff, but it must be admitted that this man's philosophy gave him stamina, made him fearless, and completely at home with nature.

Raymond Nakai, feeling the need for the establishment of an institution devoted to adult education, proposed in his inaugural address in 1967, the establishment of a community college or "Navajo Academy" on the reservation, saying:

If the tribe is to advance, the community college is extremely necessary; if we are to find a place under the sun, then this is the way to do it. Today the tribe is getting more and more sophisticated and the need for education is ever expanding.

In 1970, the Navajo Tribal Council passed a budget which included an appropriation of $250,000 for the Navajo Community College. In 1972, the college had 656 full-time students, including members of 12 other Indian tribes. The entrance requirements are quite different from those of most community colleges, which demand that students have earned a high school diploma before entrance. At the Navajo Community College, no formal education is required to qualify for admittance.

110

Adult Indians learn to read and write in English, and they may choose from a diverse offering of courses including silver-smithing and rug-weaving.

If this full approach to education had been taken before the advent of the tragic Pearl Harbor bombing, recruiting and training of Navajos in communications would have been far easier.

In addition to a paucity of educational opportunities, the Navajo faced other serious personal problems, such as wide-spread unemployment, on his return from war. One code talker says that the better jobs were always assigned to the Anglos. One of the talkers expressed his bitterness in a personal letter dated June 6, 1946, to Philip Johnston. It reads, in part, as follows:

The situation out in the Navajoland is very bad and we as vets of World War II are doing everything we can to aid our poor people. We went to Hell and back for what? For the people back here in America to tell us we can't vote!! Can't do this! Can't do that!, because you don't pay taxes and are not citizens!! We did not say we were not citizens when we volunteered for service against the ruthless and treacherous enemies, the Japs and Germans! Why?

He added a tribute to Mr. Johnston: "You will never know just how much you have done for the final great Victory being won, and the part your Navajos played to bring that Victory will never be known to America and her people at home."

What about the spirit of "patriotism" among the Navajos? On being asked, one code talker replied that the tribe does not have a word that actually means *patriotism*. "But during World War II," he said, "we were fighting for *our country*. *Then*, we were being attacked—as close as Pearl Harbor! The enemy was headed this way and we had to stop them. If someone is trying to take something away from us, we fight back. If this is what you call *patriotism*, then we are very patriotic!"

Awards came into the reservation in surprising numbers:

the Purple Heart, Silver Star, Bronze Star and Distinguished Flying Cross. One Navajo, who had been a tail gunner, had downed five Nazi planes. His ship was found to have 400 machine gun bullets embedded in it after one run over Frankfurt.

Of course, *all* races embrace men who are much better losers than winners—men who lose their composure when great success settles on their shoulders, but who are staunch under defeat. One Navajo won honors in the war, which so unsettled him that he had serious domestic trouble. An acquaintance of the man's wife desperately sought help by writing to the commanding officer of the signal training battalion to which the man had been attached:

Dear Commander:

I don't know I do rite in writin you this but no harm try. It about Big Bill ——————, can he be kept from comin home to he family, he was a fine guy till he got to be Marine, got big Head so many stripes on sleeve and decorate in front, first time come home got heap drunk, was maybe sick, cold not so bad, no want go back, next time staid over got wife take back, and made lie for him, she no like, she scared of him, all time want take car, her need live 1/4 mile out of town, she work hard, he all time send for money, talk he got woman, want car is talk, last week sends from town off far, her come after him, she no money, no gas, no go, he cot ride, made hell all time, argue, argue, car, money, he hit her maby broke nose, black both eyes, kick her round, he sure bad umbra, now take car, no paid for, how he pay, she works for his two chilen and one with till school out, and he put other woman fore her for spite. Bill no not me I get this from friends, they say fraid we write, he kill them and her maby. I going way tomorrow, try not let him know where, you get these army police here, maby you say they told. Her land woman for over year, I sure will back this up.

Mrs. B——————

No like bad man buse woman.

Seeing the Pacific area whetted the appetite for travel for one of the initial group of talkers. One day in the schoolroom, after his return, he was reading about China, when he suddenly found himself very restless. Why read about it when he might be able to *see* it? He reenlisted in the Marine Corps and asked to be sent to China. His wish was granted. He was assigned to the signal corps and was sent with a ceasefire team of the army into the land about which he had dreamed! Here he served as a communicator in contact with division headquarters in Peking. When the Communists began to activate their forces and the army was pushed out, he returned to the United States to resume the pursuit of his education.

Many of the talkers went to work officially for the Bureau of Indian Affairs, and some are now engineers, construction supervisors, interpreters, public relations experts, etc. Many took advantage of government aid and went on into higher education and eventually the professions—law, teaching, etc.

One young man who served in the navy rather than as a code talker is mentioned here in connection with "the return of the Navajo," because of the way in which he distinguished himself. He took part in the second sea battle of the Philippines, Guadalcanal, Attu, Makin, Tarawa and other engagements. After his release from the service, he sought employment with the Navajo Ordnance Depot at Bellemont, Arizona, west of Flagstaff. In addition to his depot job, he conducted a daily radio program over Station KCLS in Flagstaff for ten years.

Feeling intensely the need for Navajo education and the tribe's preparation for the modern world that had been opened to them after World War II, he began to prepare actively for a career of service to his people. In 1963, Raymond Nakai was elected chairman of the Navajo Tribe.

In his inaugural address, he pointed out the fact that half of the adult population of the tribe was deprived of the vote for national candidates because of state literacy laws, and that the average Navajo's income was less than half that of the average American.

This former shepherd boy envisioned great things for his people, as he declared:

It is a better world we have to build. It is one in which every Navajo shall stand erect beside his fellow Americans as an equal among equals. Councilors and friends, the tools are ready and the task tremendous. Let us now go to work together.

Chapter Nine

HONORING THE CODE TALKERS

The Search

. . . Tom-toms are beating and smoke signals are spiraling.

A quarter of a century after the last wave of Marines had hit the beaches, the last foxhole had been dug, the last mortar shell had hit its mark with deadly accuracy, and the Japanese had made their last-ditch stand before surrendering, General Clifton B. Cates's Fighting Fourth Marine Division began to make plans for their 22nd annual reunion. It would be a time to renew acquaintances and relive moments shared in the Central and South Pacific.

After World War II, two marines of the Fourth Division, Jerry Pines and Frank Blanchard, had an idea for a monument to the men who did not return and to those who were severely wounded: a scholarship fund for the education of their children. (This concept of service through scholarship funds was later adopted by other Marine division associations.) Reunions of the Fourth Marine Division since then have taken on the extra dimension of the business of perpetuating scholarship funds.

At previous get-togethers, commanding officers of various regiments, and other individuals who had distinguished themselves, had been singled out to be honored in a very special way. Lee Cannon, press secretary for the Fourth Division, was chairman for the upcoming occasion, which was to be held in Chicago. He turned over in his mind thoughts of the people he knew who had served significantly in some way, but who might not otherwise be honored. As an amateur student of

115

Indian lore, he was aware of the contribution of the Navajo code talkers, and thought that this might be an ideal time to confer upon them the honor they so richly merited.

It has been said (by one of their own) that serving their country at a time of crisis when the future of their beloved homeland was at stake, was a duty to be done, and one for which they expected no reward. The purification ceremonies on their return served to disentangle them from memories of the horrors of war and from the pangs of a tortured conscience. That was it! It was all over! Now it was time to get on with the business of living, back with their own people. However, it was the thought of Mr. Cannon and others of the Fourth Division that the insignia of courage and bravery under stress had been placed on the breasts of countless other deserving men; so why not decorate these warriors who had been invaluable to the Marines all over the Pacific? Not only would the Fourth Division have the high honor of decorating these brave communicators, but in addition, the gesture might serve to call the public's attention to their courageous service —a service no other group could have contributed. It was hoped that no more could it be said (quoting the code talker's letter to Mr. Johnston) that "the part your Navajos played to bring Victory will never be known to America and her people at home."

The idea of carrying out an Indian Heritage theme and honoring a representative number of the code talkers at the final banquet of the reunion struck fire with the forty-two men and women in the Chicago chapter of the association. Clayton L. Caston, CWO, USMC, Ret., president of the association, was in full agreement with the plan.

The first problem was *finding* these men—after 25 years. Lieutenant Colonel Walter Bixby and Colonel James Godbold were given the task of publicizing the plan to honor the code talkers, and he and his Marine associates launched the search through Mr. W. J. MacFarland, chief of the Office of Information of the Bureau of Indian Affairs, *The Leatherneck,*

The Navajo Times, the *Amerindian*, the *Indian Record*, a monthly put out by the Department of the Interior, and through the fantastically effective "moccasin telegraph."

The following article is an example of the kind of thing that appeared in publications that were often read by the Navajos. This one came out in the *Navajo Times* on April 17, 1969:

Tom-toms are beating and smoke signals are spiraling skyward in search of the Navajo code talkers of the 4th Division.

These Marines of American Indian heritage will be the honored guests when the men of the Fighting Fourth Marine Division Association gather in Chicago June 25-28 for their 22nd annual reunion.

In almost every operation during World War II, through the Solomons, in the Marianas, at Peleliu and Iwo Jima, the Navajo signalmen confounded the enemy with their unbreakable code.

Now more than a score of years later, the search is underway to locate these Navajos of the 4th Division who contributed so magnificently to victory.

They will step front and center at the final banquet in the Sheraton-Chicago Hotel on Saturday night, June 28, to receive a salute and accolade from their fellow Marines.

At that time a specifically struck medallion on an authentic Indian beaded band will be placed around the neck (Medal of Honor style) of each Navajo who served in the 4th Division.

Because of the tremendous significance of the event, the 1st, 2nd, 3rd, 5th and 6th divisions have been invited to select one member of their own Navajo code talkers to represent their organization at the 4th Division's reunion and also receive the same medal.

Of the total 540 Navajos enlisted by the Marine Corps, 420 qualified as code talkers. Few experiments in World War II proved more successful than the Navajo code talkers.

The Chicago committee, headed by Lee Cannon, chairman, George Mazarakos, executive secretary, and Colonel Joseph

117

McCarthy, M.O.H., met with members of the Navajo tribe, among whom was Peter MacDonald, destined to become chairman of the Navajo Tribal Council a few years later. Lloyd L. House, the first Navajo to serve in the Arizona legislature, was selected by tribe members, to serve as liaison between the Navajos and the Chicago reunion committee. The Navajo Tribal Council accepted the responsibility of choosing fifteen Navajo code talkers from the Fourth Marine Division, and one each from the First, Second, Third, Fifth and Sixth, to be honored at the reunion.

The response was heartwarming. Officers who remembered the names of code talkers under their command sent information. One man sent a list of names and addresses (as of 1945) of twenty-eight Navajos who had been in the Fourth Signal Company. Letters from code talkers themselves began to trickle in.

With the search underway, the committee began to make arrangements to bring these men to Chicago by plane. Brigadier General Jay W. Hubbard, director of the Division of Information at Marine Headquarters, assured the committee of his wholehearted cooperation in their plans to honor the code talkers, and named Colonel Ruth Broe as special projects officer to represent the Corps. Plans were finally set in motion for a transport to pick up the Navajos at Albuquerque and fly them to Chicago on June 25, the first day of the reunion.

Invitations were sent out to men in high positions in the nation, related in some way to the project, and the transportation arrangements and hotel accommodations for the special guests were made. Marines were assigned to act as special hosts to the Navajos in Chicago, and those in charge now began to arrange for the right decoration to be given to each code talker on that important occasion.

The Medallion

. . . A Dream—A Reality

Ira Hayes, His Dream—His Reality is a painting done by

Ira Hayes, His Dream—His Reality, by Joe Ruiz Grandee. Copyright © 1969 by Joe Ruiz Grandee. All rights reserved.

the artist Joe Ruiz Grandee, that has attracted nationwide attention. Ira Hayes, a Pima Indian, was, as was noted in American newspapers across the land, one of the men who raised the flag on Mount Suribachi in Iwo Jima. He was caught by the camera of Joe Rosenthal, Associated Press photographer, in a poignant scene at a strategic moment in history.

Arthur Stanton, veteran Marine, friend of Hayes (whom he characterized as a "loner"), had asked Mr. Grandee to paint this picture. He spoke with admiration of the man who had dreamed with envy of his ancestors, who once roamed the vast plains of the great West, proud and free.

The large painting depicts Hayes, dressed in the hunting regalia of his tribe, astride an Indian pony. To his left and in the background in a glowing mist are those unforgettable men, victoriously planting the stars and stripes on Mount Suribachi.

The painting was presented to General Wallace M. Greene, Jr., Commandant of the Marine Corps, on February 19, 1965, during ceremonies to commemorate the twentieth anniversary of the historic landing on Iwo Jima. The painting was hung in Marine Corps Headquarters, and later transferred to the Marine Corps Museum at Quantico, Virginia.

What painting could possibly be more significant as the basis for the design on a medallion to honor the Indian Marine? Mr. Cannon, calling Mr. Grandee to ask his permission to use it on the medallion design, received a quick affirmative response.

The Franklin Mint in Yeadon, Pennsylvania, designed and struck the medallion in bronze—an amazingly faithful replica in an entirely different medium. It depicts Ira Hayes and the Suribachi scene in sharp relief on the face of the medallion, and the symbol of the Fourth Marine Division on the reverse side. It is one-fourth inch in thickness, and three inches in diameter.

To support the heavy decorations, rawhide thongs eighteen inches long and strung with red, white and blue Indian beads,

Medallion struck from *Ira Hayes*.

were ordered from a center of the Southern Plains Indians at Anadarko, Oklahoma.

On the occasion of the commemorative banquet, *Ira Hayes, His Dream—His Reality*, hung over the heads of the recipients of the medallion!

The following was written by Joy Schultz to appear opposite a print of the painting in her book, *The West Still Lives*:[16]

> Wear it with pride, you gallant few
> Who live to remind a world
> Of a mountain, a war, a handful of men
> Who saw a flag unfurled.
> Iwo Jima! Who can forget
> What a free world found to praise
> As brave Marines lift a flag aloft?
> One an Indian—Ira Hayes,
> Reservation his home, poor his lot,
> He harbored a dream that he
> Could have lived as his fathers before him lived:
> Daring—and brave—and free.
> He wanted to live in a day long passed
> That lives in the Indian's story;
> On an isle in World War II
> He found his moment of glory.
> The man is gone, but the dream lives on
> And it looms on history's scene,
> Ira Hayes and the stars and stripes
> A hero—an Indian—Marine!
> In some far happier hunting ground
> Where dead chiefs their mounts can tether,
> There is a place for Marine Ira Hayes—
> The man and the dream together.

The Ceremony

. . . Step front and center.

The Navajo warriors arrived in Chicago (land of the Wild Onion) on June 25. As they deplaned, they were met by Harry

16. Joy Schultz, *The West Still Lives*, Dallas: Heritage Press, 1970. Reprinted by permission of Western Art of America.

Navajos are feted at Independence Hall in Chicago.

Larrison, Chicago chairman of the Honor Committee, Gunnery Sergeant G. R. Smith, Corps photographer, and the Drum and Bugle Corps of the Fourth Marine Air Wing. The Navajos were feted from the moment they arrived. Their first stop in the big city was at Independence Hall, where the president of the institution, Dr. Sidney L. DeLove, greeted them with a hot buffet, and showed them his collection of early Americana, including guns and priceless documents. They were then taken to the Executive House, which, as one of them said, was to be their "home away from hogan."

During their stay, they were given a sightseeing tour of the city, were entertained at a powwow sponsored by Indians of Chicago at the American Indian Center, and were photographed and interviewed by newsmen. Many people and representatives of institutions requested the honor of hosting the visiting Indians at luncheons and other social events.

The big day was June 28, which began with a colorful parade in downtown Chicago. Members of the Fourth Marine Division marched briskly down the avenue, with many of the code talkers in their traditional costumes. Memorial services held at Pioneer Court were the climax of the parade.

At the luncheon at Executive House, the code talkers honored Harry Larrison and his wife, Mary, their hosts during their stay in Chicago, by presenting them with a handsome Bolo tie of silver and turquoise.

The event for which the Navajos had left the reservation was the banquet. It was a colorful affair in an elegant setting, with high-ranking officers and distinguished citizens at the speaker's table.

Colonel Joseph McCarthy, representing Richard J. Daley, mayor of Chicago, welcomed the Marines to the city, greetings were extended from General Leonard F. Chapman, Jr., Commandant of the Marine Corps, through his representative, Brigadier General Robert P. Keller of Glenview Naval Air Station, and greetings from the Fourth Marine Division through Brigadier General William J. Weinstein.

Navajos pose before statue of Marine in Chicago.

General Clifton B. Cates presents medallion to Robert L. Bennett, former commissioner of Indian Affairs.

126

A lithograph of Navajo code talkers was presented to Robert L. Bennett, former commissioner of Indian Affairs, by John Fabion, Fourth Marine Division combat artist, professor emeritus of art at Chicago Art Institute.

Richard T. Burress, deputy counsel, representing President Richard Nixon, read a message from the commander-in-chief, and conveyed personal greetings to the code talkers. Mr. Burress had served as a lieutenant in the Fourth Marine Division in the Iwo Jima campaign. Anthony Lincoln, then director of the Navajo Tribe, responded for the Honorable Raymond Nakai, then chairman of the Navajo nation, by thanking the Commandant of the Marine Corps and all those assembled for the honor to be conferred upon the code talkers.

Mr. Cannon, referring to the "quiet heroes who have made this a most memorable reunion," asked Mr. Larrison to present the American Indian Marine awards.

In an atmosphere of charged emotion, Mr. Cannon asked the men to step front and center as their names were called to receive the decoration for meritorious service in communications. The name with serial number, and the battalion, regiment and division in which each served was called out amid tumultuous applause. General officers took turns placing the medallions around the necks of the Indian warriors.

As the ceremony proceeded, a strange sense of true brotherhood could be felt, coupled with a profound pride in achievement in the service of the nation. Many of those present were unable to suppress tears. After the last of the code talkers of the Fourth Division had been decorated, Mr. Cannon said, in a voice reflecting his own depth of feeling, "These men are quiet; they kept their trust; they are Fourth Division heroes— every one of them! To them our heartiest congratulations!"

Others who received awards were representatives of the other five Marine divisions, Colonel Ruth Broe, Corporal Lillian C. Namingha (Hopi-Tewa) for all women Marines of Indian heritage, Chief Warren Sanky, Fourth Tank Battalion, of Oklahoma, on behalf of other American Indian tribes who

Lee Cannon (right) presents award plaque to Joe Ruiz Grandee, artist, whose painting, *Ira Hayes, His Dream —His Reality,* was used as the design for the medallion.

Brigadier General Robert P. Keller (right) presents award medallion to Anthony Lincoln, then director of the Navajo Tribe.

Recipients of the award medallion at the reunion banquet.

Colonel Ruth Broe congratulates Corporal Lillian C. Namingha on receipt of the medallion.

129

served during World War II with the Marines, and Anthony Lincoln, for Chairman Raymond Nakai.

Mr. Cannon related briefly the way in which he had heard about Philip Johnston's place in the origin of the Navajo code. During the initial stages of the reunion search for the code talkers, letters and telephone calls came to him in Chicago, the gist of which was, "How about Philip Johnston?" (He got busy, and through Harry Larrison, located the man in California.)

Now at the reunion, Mr. Cannon requested that Mr. Burress, the President's representative, officiate in the presentation of the medallion to this man who had initiated the project. Completely taken by surprise, this experienced platform man was at a loss for words. He responded to the totally unexpected honor by singing in Navajo the Marine Hymn (with the help of the Indians present)—the translation made by Jimmy Kelly King at Camp Elliott in 1943. He then exclaimed in the tongue of the code talkers, "The Navajo Marines are great!"

Frank Brookhouser, in his book, *This Was Your War*, writes in a pensive mood of the annual reunions with his army buddies. Part of his description follows:

> The reunions are important to us. There is a great deal of laughter. There are a host of shared memories as scenes and incidents are recalled in the mellow atmosphere.... There they sit ... laughing once more at a one-time funny scene, recreated loudly and brought vividly to light, speaking suddenly in total recall of little towns important now only to the people who live in them, and to the guys who were once there in their lives, in mud and snow and rain and black nights filled only with the steady ominous drone of planes overhead and hushed voices below.[17]

All reunions of men who have served their country together have a common ground, and a somber note that lingers. But

17. Frank Brookhouser, ed., *This Was Your War*, New York: Doubleday, 1960, pp. 11-12.

Richard T. Burress, deputy counsel, representing President Richard Nixon, presents medallion to Philip Johnston.

the twenty-second reunion of the Fourth Marine Division had an additional dimension. Walter J. Hickel, Secretary of the Interior, expressed it in a telegram to the reunion committee:

This year your reunion will be especially significant because of the richly merited recognition you are giving to the American Indian Marines who served with the Fighting Fourth in World War II. The Navajo Code Talkers who served with the Fourth made a unique contribution to your division and to Marine Corps history. The presentation of medallions to these veterans will honor not only them, but the Indian people throughout the country.

On June 25, Robert N. Huey, officer-in-charge at the Industrial Development Field Office of the Bureau of Indian Affairs, sent this message:

It is most gratifying to observe the show of nostalgia for a job well done by the members of this Division during World War II. It is especially pleasing to me, on this reunion occasion 25 years later, that you have chosen to honor your brothers in combat—the Navajo Code Talkers who, with flying colors, so indelibly planted their efforts on the hearts and minds of Americans everywhere.

A few weeks after the reunion, Mr. Cannon received this letter from John B. Richardson, chief of Social Service of the Public Health Service Indian Hospital at Albuquerque:

It has been brought to my attention by one of our staff members that the Fighting Fourth Marine Division recently had a reunion . . . I was shown a June copy of *The Leatherneck* that described what was to occur.

What interested us was the awards to be given to the Navajo Marines who participated in the code division. It related how medals would be given to those men because of their contribution to the war by delivering radio messages in Navajo—a language the Japanese couldn't figure out.

132

Pfc. Frank Toledo receiving award medallion at Public Health Service Indian Hospital at Albuquerque.

Left to right, Vice-chairman Navajo Tribal Council Wilson C. Skeet, Chairman Navajo Tribal Council Peter MacDonald, Brigadier General Leslie Brown, U.S. Marine Corps., Lee Cannon, Fourth Marine Division Association. (*Department of the Interior, Bureau of Indian Affairs.*)

133

Pictured in that article was Pfc. Frank Toledo. He did not attend your reunion, because he is being treated for tuberculosis.

Is it possible for him to still receive recognition and an award? He does not know about this inquiry, but it is felt that this would encourage him while he is hospitalized.

Mr. Cannon responded, "It will be an honor for us to pay recognition to Mr. Toledo, and to see to it that a Marine unit in Albuquerque presents him with his medallion with full honors."

Marine Corps Headquarters, through the cooperation of Colonel Ruth Broe, and under the able direction of Captain Richard Hodory and Staff Sergeant Jerry D. Scoggins, set up an honoring ceremony in front of the hospital with all the staff and patients in attendance, and with three television stations and the local newspapers represented. The award was made by Lieutenant Colonel Nevin E. Dayvault in an impressive atmosphere. That evening all of the television stations carried the story in their newscasts, and newspapers gave it space.

The business of making awards in honor of the code talkers was not yet finished. Another chapter was enacted at the twenty-third annual tribal fair in Window Rock, Arizona, on Labor Day. The *Gallup* (NM) *Independent* carried this story on September 2, 1969:

On Saturday night, the grandstand was full to overflowing. Before the performance there was a special memorial service for all Navajo war dead.

Chairman Raymond Nakai received a medallion and plaque on behalf of the Tribe, and the Navajo Code Talkers, from Sgt. Lee Cannon of the Fourth Marine Division Association.

After thanking Sgt. Cannon, Chairman Nakai said, "Many people have asked us why we fight the white man's wars. Our answer is always that *we are proud to be Ameri-*

can, and we are proud to be American Indians.... The American Indian always stands ready when his country needs him!"

About two years later, January 5, 1971, the medallion honoring the code talkers was presented by Lee Cannon to the newly-elected chairman, Peter MacDonald, and the vice-chairman, Wilson C. Skeet, both of whom served their nation in the Sixth Division as code talkers!

Chapter Ten

CENTURY OF ACHIEVEMENT

... We are not afraid of hard trails.

The Navajo Country, home of the famed code talkers, is a startling picture of contrasts between the primitive past and the sleek, bright present. There is the hogan as Kit Carson saw it, and the modern house with all the conveniences; the basket-weaver and the smart young career woman; the man who trudges many miles for supplies, and the man who sits in his spanking-new truck and spins long distances in minutes.

The chic daughter, wearing the latest fashion, shops at the supermarket with her mother, who is wearing the colorful traditional long full skirt and velveteen blouse, a costume which is said to carry the design of the apparel worn by the wives of white officers at Fort Sumner a hundred years ago. Well-groomed officials in agency and government offices listen to the problems of elderly Navajo men, who are wearing their long black or grey hair clubbed in back.

The people are attempting to hold on to the best of both worlds, sometimes finding themselves beset by problems and frustration. Some have said, "We don't know who we are!" They are torn between the old beliefs and those taught in mission schools and churches; between traditional attitudes and modern philosophy.

Some hail the triumph of the astronauts with fervent admiration; others feel that the basic laws of nature have been violated by going to the moon and that we will reap disaster— that this intrusion may affect rainfall, vegetation and life itself.

The Navajo to whom time of day means only morning, noon, afternoon, and evening, must re-gear his entire concept when he punches a time-clock. He must change his concept of ownership from the plan of family rights to individual rights of possession, when he enters the white-dominated society.

The insistence of the leaders of Navajo life that members of the tribe be allowed to be themselves, rather than a people modeled after the white man, is strongly taking root. One Indian student at Stanford University said,

> The goal, it seems to me, is to produce kids who can hold their own in the mainstream of Indian culture, and those who will be tribal leaders on their reservations. If the Indians are to maintain their culture they will need doctors and lawyers (and other professional men) who are dually oriented. This is a process of acculturation, not assimilation. We want to maintain our own culture but get the white man's skills to help us do so.

Educators are now beginning to see that they have been wrong in punishing children for speaking Navajo in school. To keep the ancestral legends alive, old storytellers go to the dormitories of the boarding schools to relate them to the students, just as their parents or grandparents once told them in the hogans during the long winter nights in the past.

A small brochure published by the Navajo Facility, Pomona Division of General Dynamics, entitled, "The Electronic Age Comes to Navajoland" says:

> One of the "emerging nations" of the world is that of the Navajo Indians. Awakened by the heroic service of their tribesmen in World War II and Korea, and plagued by a lack of post-war job opportunities, the Navajo Tribal Council has taken the lead in bringing about an industrial and economic revolution for its people. Navajos, traditionally skilled in the arts of weaving and jewelry-making, are now training their young to master the complexities involved in the building of electronic hardware.

Through wise planning the Navajo Tribal Council has utilized royalties from its oil wells and other mineral resources to finance and develop Navajo-owned businesses for the collective betterment of the people. The Navajos have invested heavily in the future by providing land, buildings and skilled personnel. Industries like General Dynamics operate the facilities, supply the work and the technical and administrative know-how. Such working together provides necessary economic assistance, new hope and opportunity to the Navajo nation. Its people have a renewed sense of purpose and personal dignity.

The Navajo Facility of the Pomona Division of General Dynamics is located at Fort Defiance, Arizona, about 35 miles northwest of Gallup, New Mexico. A completely air-conditioned concrete and steel building, built, and owned by the Navajo Tribe, contains offices, a machine shop, and production and test areas. It is completely equipped with the newest, most modern tools and machinery. New employees receive instruction in soldering, electronic welding, wiring and assembly techniques.

Mr. E. J. Balbos, Employee Relations administrator, stated that minimum educational requirements in the plant are graduation from the eighth grade. Some employees have been students at boarding schools, where they lived with the Anglo society. Some have strongly traditional parents. Most of them have specific material goals, such as better things for the home. Approximately nine-tenths of the employees are Navajos.

Another successful project in this area of industry is Fairchild Semiconductor's big electronics plant at Shiprock, New Mexico. The million-dollar installation was built by the tribe and leased to Fairchild. In 1972, its employees numbered 750, only 24 of whom were non-Navajo.

Another major development in industry is the Navajo Forest Products Industries, located at Navajo, New Mexico. It all started in 1888, when a small mill was built on the Navajo reservation to cut lumber for Indian Service buildings, such as

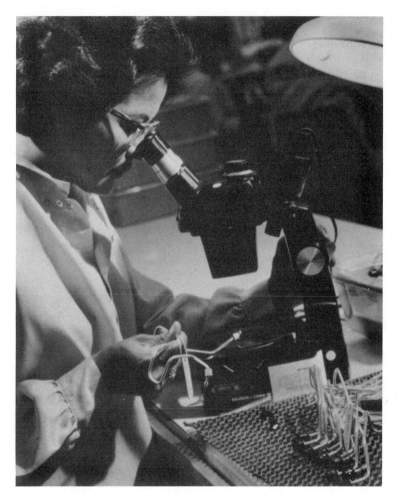

Navajo woman at work in the General Dynamics plant at Fort Defiance, Arizona.

schools, office buildings, missions and agency homes.

In 1929, the Navajo reservation branch of forestry was created and given the responsibility of managing existing small government mills along with forest management. In 1953, the Tribal Council and the commissioner of the Bureau of Indian Affairs, jointly approved a plan for timber management. Three years later, outside consultants were brought in to advise on formation of expanded lumber manufacturing facilities. In 1966, a bark processing plant was set up to produce humus, pebble bark, acorn bark, and jumbo bark for agricultural uses, bed plants, shrubbery and ground cover. Chips were also processed, to be used in manufacturing prefab homes.

In 1969, a second boiler and electrical generating plant were installed. By utilizing excess wood-waste for fuel, the new facilities provided steam power and electrical energy for the Navajo Tribal Utility Enterprises. Today Navajo pine is sold throughout the Southwest, and as far east as Michigan, Indiana and Ohio.

Development of agriculture is of prime importance to tribal leaders. Over the years, large numbers of irrigation projects have been completed to assist the farmers. A Farm Training Program is jointly sponsored by the Navajo tribe and the Bureau of Indian Affairs. A grazing committee is mapping out areas for families to use for their sheep and cattle. The committee sets up regulations to be followed by all stock owners. An advisory group also regulates homesite status along with land use.

In 1967, the Navajos recognized the need for a retail store to sell meats, groceries, hardware, department store items and auto supplies at the lowest possible prices. They asked the FedMart Corporation to build such a store in their capital. They had made a feasibility study concerning the annual retail sales potential at Window Rock, a study that came up with the surprising figure of $4 million.

FedMart's vice-president, Robert E. Price, was dubious at

Dry-kiln foreman at the Navajo Tribe's $6.5 million sawmill. (Photo by Don Erb, Public Relations Department, Santa Fe Railway.)

Sawmill at Navajo, New Mexico, owned by the Navajo Tribe.

first, for there seemed to be nothing promising at Window Rock for a discount store business. But the company agreed to build a 33,000-square-foot facility. The Navajos invested about $65,000 and FedMart about $150,000. The tribe owns the store and leases it to FedMart, a policy maintained in all non-Navajo-directed operations on the reservation.

The store opened on November 1, 1968. Today the annual volume of sales has soared into the multi-million-dollar bracket.

The modern Window Rock Motor Inn quietly opened its doors in March, 1970, with fifty rooms leased to an Anglo businessman for a motel and forty rooms to the Indian Health Service as offices. The motel was soon buzzing with business. It is a comfortable, attractive hostelry for visitors to the area or guests of the tribal government, with an excellent dining room and coffee shop, and facilities for special events. During the first month of operation, a number of conferences (including an educators' meeting) were held there. Young Navajo men and women who have spent little time in the white man's world were trained by the manager and a capable executive housekeeper to keep books, register guests, keep the place spotlessly clean, serve food, and to make a visit to the inn a pleasant and enjoyable experience.

It is no surprise that Kentucky Fried Chicken has found its way to Window Rock. The people now have some paved roads, hospitals, tribal parks, and recreation centers. They rely heavily for their financing on natural resources such as oil, uranium, helium and coal.

Raymond Nakai (chairman of the Navajo Tribal Council from 1963 through 1970) spoke eloquently to the author of plans for the future of the nation, in terms of the expansion of educational facilities, and further industrialization, and added, "We boast of unpolluted air, and a place where man can get closer to nature—where he can go and commune and really 'get unwound.' " The tribe does not intend to permit the establishment of industries that might in any way interfere

142

Honorable Raymond Nakai, chairman of the Navajo Tribal Council, 1963-1970.

with the *status quo*. Men who wish to build factories must agree to install filter systems to keep the air clean.

Looking back to the opening of the Centennial Year, one hundred years after the signing of the Peace Treaty of 1868, it is remembered that Mr. Nakai delivered a stirring address, a portion of which follows:

The Century of Progress which we commemorate has not been an easy one hundred years. It was initiated by the tragic and heartbreaking "long march" from Ft. Sumner. It marked a struggle of a proud people, accustomed to roam unfettered over the vast expanses of this great western United States. It reflects the slow, but steady progress of our people to this very moment. However difficult has been our struggle, never was the faith of the Navajo people the least bit diminished in their ultimate place in our society. Never did the Navajo despair. Always, he sought and fought for a better way of life. All in all, this past one hundred years does reflect great progress on the part of our people. But we are at the beginning of our true development. I shall not be here when the second centennial of the Navajo Nation is commemorated, but let me here give the next hundred years a name.

As the first has been called a Century of Progress, let the second be called a Century of Achievement. We are, indeed, on the threshold of great achievements for our people in the fields of education, industrial development, and economic well-being. The next decades will witness giant steps forward in these areas. Yes, we are on a "long march" again —a march forward and upward—a march toward achievement for all that is good for our people.

It shall require the best in all of us to reach our goal, for our sights are high, and we will not be content for mere modest achievements. Let us resolve to make this next one hundred years a great century for our people, so that our children's children, in the year 2068, can announce with pride—"This past one hundred years has been, indeed, a century of Great Achievement."

Peter MacDonald, inaugurated January 5, 1971, as chairman of the Tribal Council, has pledged to continue in the direction set by his predecessor, Mr. Nakai. He says that his own life story is a good example of what Navajos are going to have to do to achieve their aims.

He was born on the reservation near Four Corners, a meeting place for the states of Arizona, New Mexico, Colorado and Utah. He was given the Navajo name that means "He who clasps hands with strength"—a name suggested by a white man at the trading post.

His parents were poor, and neither of them spoke English. His father died when he was only two years old, and his mother and the four children went to live with his grandfather.

When Peter's mother took him to school for the first time, the teacher asked the child's last name. Peter had always been called by the one name only and his mother suddenly came up with the Navajo term that means "many whiskers" (his grandfather's name). The word sounded like "Donald" to the teacher and she registered him under the name Peter Donald. When the little boy learned that well-known song, "Old MacDonald Had a Farm," he decided to change his name to Peter MacDonald.

When he was 12, he left school to herd sheep, and later to work at a sawmill in Dolores, Colorado. Here he heard that a railroad was hiring men on the line all the way to Oregon. Being only 14 1/2 at the time, he was not eligible for one of these jobs, for which the applicants had to be 18 years of age. To take care of this little deterrent, he went to the Selective Service Board for a draft card, giving his age as 18. About six weeks later in Oregon, the government caught up with him and he was drafted for service. At the age of 15 he became a Marine, and not long after saw service in the Pacific.

On his return, he was able to finish high school in a period of nine months. He eventually graduated from the University of Oklahoma with a degree in electrical engineering. The degree led him to a job with the Hughes Aircraft Corporation, and subsequently a position as executive in the Polaris missile program.

Chairman MacDonald is the grandson of Lefty Curley Hair and Little Grandmother, who were among those who made the Long Walk. The pull of the past and his own people made him agree to leave his fine position in California and return to the reservation to take a federal post. He was active in the affairs of the Navajo nation for eight years prior to his election to its highest post.

Mr. MacDonald says he would like to see a "yellow pages section" in the telephone directory for Navajos, including listings for food stores, filling stations, dry-cleaning establishments, car dealers, movie theaters, clothing stores, Coca-Cola bottling plants, barber shops, and motels—owned by Navajos and employing Navajos. In order to accomplish these goals he foresees two necessary changes:

(1) A stronger emphasis on young Navajos getting a sound education to take over responsible jobs in private business; and to do that they also need practical experience in tough competition off the reservation.

(2) The government must institute economic aid with a permanent effect. The three primary needs are a major roadbuilding project, the bringing of electric power into all of the vast area of the reservation and a similar undertaking to make ample water available for manufacturing.

On July 9 and 10 (1971), sixty-five former code talkers convened at the Tribal Museum in Window Rock, Arizona, for the purpose of organizing an association, as well as enjoying the reunion with buddies who had been under fire with them almost thirty years before, as communicators in the Pacific.

The meeting was co-sponsored by the Center of Western History in Utah, and Martin Link, curator of the Navajo Tribal Museum, along with Ted Evans, director of Veterans Affairs for the tribe.

A spirit of excitement and camaraderie prevailed. Philip

Peter MacDonald at his inauguration as chairman of the Navajo Tribal Council. (*UPI*)

Johnston was there to spark memories of experiences at Camp Elliott and Camp Pendleton.

At one session devoted to organization, John Benally was elected chairman, James Nakai, vice-chairman, and William McCabe, secretary-treasurer. A member from each of the six divisions was then elected to the board.

The first meeting of the Navajo code talkers association was scheduled to be held at Window Rock on Veterans Day in the fall of 1971.

To test their skills in code talking, an event took place with the aid of the Marine post in Albuquerque. Camp was set up on the hill behind the museum (now facetiously called C Ration Hill). Most of the code talkers congregated on this hill while a small group was deployed to another hill about a mile away. Messages in code, such as "Hill 182 was taken 0600 A.M. this date," were sent by field telephone. If the receivers understood the message they would give the sender the "roger" and repeat the message in English. The last code talker to test his skill sent this message: "May the Navajo Nation endure for all time! In God we trust!"

The country as a whole is becoming increasingly aware of the vital place of the Navajo tribe in the national life, and many have belatedly discovered their contribution in winning the victory in World War II.

Preceding the annual Navajo Tribal Fair, held September 8-12 (1971), President Richard Nixon sent the following message to Peter MacDonald, Chairman of the Navajo Tribal Council:

> The Navajo Tribal Fair has become in the quarter-century of its history, one of the most colorful and popular events of its kind. It is a continuing reminder to all Americans of the contributions that the Navajo Tribe has made to the vitality of our cultural heritage, and it reflects the economic progress of your people.
>
> In my Message to Congress last year relating to Indian

Sergeant Jerry Scroggins and Philip Johnston on C Ration Hill, during the Code Talkers' reunion.

Martin Link, curator of the Navajo Tribal Museum, gets instructions on how to operate a walky-talky from code-talkers Merril Sandoval and Teddy Draper, at the Code Talkers' reunion.

Judge Dean Wilson sends a message during the Code Talkers' reunion; Teddy Draper assists by recording. Paul Blatchford looks on during the proceedings.

affairs, and in subsequent legislative proposals I made to the Congress, I spelled out a program of economic, educational, health and other related measures on behalf of American Indians. I take this occasion to renew my pledge of support for that legislation and every program that will give substance to the hopes this Administration shares with you for the coming of the day when all American Indians will have the fullness of opportunity that is their rightful due as citizens of this great country.

The president followed this message with one that was read during the Memorial Service for veterans (during the Tribal Fair) on the afternoon of September 11:

Since sending my greetings to you and the participants in the Navajo Tribal Fair, it has come to my attention that the occasion will feature a special tribute to the Marine Corps Navajo Indian Code Talkers. I welcome this opportunity to reinforce the best wishes I extended to you, with special personal tribute to these outstanding citizens whose successful mission earned them the gratitude and admiration of all Americans. Their resourcefulness, tenacity, integrity and courage saved the lives of countless men and women and sped the realization of peace for war-torn lands. In the finest spirit of the Marine Corps, their achievements form a proud chapter in American military history. My congratulations to them on behalf of all their fellow citizens.

On July 25, 1972, leaders of the Navajo nation met in the council chambers to hear the news they had long awaited. At this meeting, Council Chairman Peter MacDonald accepted the offer of the United States to let the Navajo people run the affairs of their own reservation.

The plan as proposed by the United States government is to give the tribe, within a period of two years, control over the $100-million-a-year operation that has up to this time been administered by the Bureau of Indian Affairs in the Department of the Interior.

President Nixon meets with Peter MacDonald, chairman of the Navajo Tribal Council. (*UPI*)

The author is reminded of the call for united effort found in a statement made by Chairman MacDonald at his inauguration (printed on the program for the ceremony): "Let us all come together in the spirit of cooperation, and move forward together into a new era of great achievements, opportunities and a better tomorrow for all."

It now appears that Navajos *can* look toward a "better tomorrow" with confidence and hope—if they all "come together" with the ardor of the veteran code talker who fervently prays that the Navajo Nation "may endure for all time!" One Indian summed it all up when he said, "We have a hard trail ahead of us, but we are not afraid of hard trails."

APPENDIX

For those readers interested in documentation of a presentation of historical events, pertinent military correspondence and certain official reports are herewith presented, references to which have been made in the body of the book. Original copies of these documents are housed in the Navajo Tribal Museum at Window Rock, Arizona.

Item I

PROPOSED PLAN FOR RECRUITING INDIAN SIGNAL CORPS PERSONNEL

1. *General.* The American Indian comprises a distinct racial subdivision, presumed by anthropologists to have migrated from Asia by way of the "land-bridge" at Bering Strait. Dates of these migrations have not been fixed, but recent excavations have disclosed human remains in association with those of the now extinct giant sloth—an indication that earlier migrations occurred more than 20,000 years ago.

Present Indian population of the United States is 361,816, comprising 180 tribes. These are divided into distinct linguistic stocks, each of whose languages has apparently evolved from a common source. The total number of tribes in the United States, Canada, and British Columbia is 230, which represents 56 linguistic stocks. The language of a tribe belonging to one linguistic stock is completely alien to that of another stock; and in most cases variations of the tongues within a linguistic stock may be so great as to be mutually unintelligible.

All Indian languages are classed as "unwritten" because no alphabets or other symbols of purely native origin are in existence. In a few cases, these aboriginal tongues have been reduced to writing by American scholars, who have developed alphabets adapted to the expression of the difficult consonants involved. A notable instance in point is the Navajo Dictionary compiled by the Franciscan Fathers of Saint Michaels, Arizona, who have also translated portions of the Bible, and written other texts in the Navajo tongue for the use of their students. Recently, the United States Bureau of Indian Affairs has inaugurated a program of writing Navajo texts for study in reservation schools. However, a fluency in reading Navajo can be acquired only by individuals who are first highly educated in English, and who, in turn, have made a profound study of Navajo, both in its spoken and written form. An illiterate Navajo is, of course, entirely unable to read his own language.

Because of the fact that a complete understanding of words and terms comprising the various Indian languages could be had only by those whose ears had been highly trained in them, these dialects would be ideally suited to communication in various branches of our armed forces. Messages sent and received between two individuals of the same tribe could not, under any circumstances, be interpreted by the enemy; conversations by telephone or short-wave radio could be carried on without possibility of disclosure to hostile forces.

2. *Tribes Available for Recruitment.* A logical approach to the problem of selection of suitable personnel for an Indian Signal Corps would be to consider the largest tribes in the United States. Reference to accompanying maps will show locations of each of the following:

Tribe	Population
Navajo	49,338
Sioux (in South Dakota)	20,670
Chippewa	17,443
Pima-Papago	11,915

The Pima and Papago tribes are so closely allied in language as to be mutually intelligible.

Percentage of literacy among the foregoing tribes would be in direct proportion to the length of time each has been in contact with educational facilities. The Chippewa would no doubt have the highest percentage, with the Sioux second, the Pima-Papago third, and the Navajo fourth. It should be noted, however, that a pre-requisite to effective service in transmitting code messages is an excellent command of both the native tongue and of the English. In some cases, individuals of a tribe which has had long contact with white residents may have largely forgotten his native tongue.

Since only a minute percentage of the foregoing tribes are college graduates, it is unlikely that 250 members of each, between the ages 21-30, would be available for recruitment. However, a fair number have attended government and public schools, and completed twelve grades, equivalent to high school. Without doubt a large majority of these would have sufficient command of both their native tongues and of English to qualify for service in the signal corps. It is also probable some individuals with even less schooling, by reason of constant use of the English language, might be qualified for signal corps service. This matter could readily be ascertained by giving each applicant an examination to show his fluency in both tongues.

3. *Recruitment of Navajo Indians.* This tribe is selected as an example of a possible plan for recruitment because of the writer's intimate knowledge of its reservation, the people, and their language. Most of the factors discussed would apply to the other three tribes in varying degrees.

With an area of 25,000 square miles, and an approximate population of 50,000, the Navajo reservation is one of the most sparsely populated sections of the United States. It is traversed by unimproved roads and trails; and many of its outlying portions are accessible only on horseback. Culturally and linguistically, the Navajo has been autonomous, and apart from surrounding white population. But in recent years, an increasing number of Navajo children have attended schools established by the government on this reservation, where they have received grammar school instruction; and a large percentage of these students have graduated from other schools of higher grades located at points remote from the reservation, where the curricula include native arts and crafts, as well as various trades and occupations taught in accredited schools throughout the United States.

Because the manner of life on the Navajo reservation provides small opportunity for educated Indians to set up a standard of living compatible with their training, a large portion of them have sought employment in government agencies and institutions, and in towns near the reservation. Therefore, an effective program to contact suitable personnel for recruitment would require publicity designed to reach every Navajo whose age and education qualifies him for service. The most important feature of such a program would be a bulletin prepared to set forth the following:

(a) That the Navajos are in a unique position to render service in the defense of the United States—a service which will be of inestimable value.

(b) That such a service would involve the transmission of messages in their own tongue, which is not understood by any other people in the world.

(c) That meritorious service in such a capacity may result in advancement in the service.

(d) That applications for enlistment are received at designated localities.

155

The best location for a central recruiting station would be at the Central Navajo Agency, Window Rock, Arizona, or Gallup, New Mexico. Secondary stations for contact of local applicants should be located at several points throughout the reservation, preferably at Tuba City, Arizona, Chin Lee, Arizona, and Shiprock, New Mexico. Special efforts should also be made to contact Navajos through government school superintendents at Leupp, Fort Defiance, Kayenta, and Keams Canyon, Arizona, and Crownpoint, New Mexico.

A considerable number of eligible applicants will also be found among the following categories:

(a) Navajos attending non-reservation government schools, such as those located at Phoenix, Arizona, and Albuquerque, New Mexico.

(b) Educated Navajos employed at the foregoing schools, and in various capacities by the government.

(c) Educated Navajos who are employed off the reservation, principally in the cities of Flagstaff, Winslow, Gallup, and Albuquerque.

(d) Navajos who have already enlisted, or have been inducted into the armed forces, who might be transferred to the Marine Corps for special training in signal work.

4. *Indian Affairs Officials.* Direct contact with the Navajo Reservation should be made through Mr. E. R. Fryer, Superintendent, Central Navajo Agency, Window Rock, Arizona. Contacts with proper authorities among the other three tribes listed can be made through the Honorable John Collier, Commissioner of Indian Affairs, Washington, D. C.

Item II

15/11-jwa

Headquarters
Amphibious Corps, Pacific Fleet
Camp Elliott, San Diego, California
March 6, 1942

From: The Commanding General
To: The Commandant, U.S. Marine Corps
Subject: Enlistment of Navajo Indians
Enclosures: (A) Brochure by Mr. Philip Johnston, with maps
            (B) Messages used in demonstration

1. Mr. Philip Johnston of Los Angeles recently offered his services to this force to demonstrate the use of Indians for the transmission of messages by telephone and voice-radio. His offer was accepted and the demonstration was held for the Commanding General and his staff.

2. The demonstration was interesting and successful. Messages were transmitted and received almost verbatim. In conducting the demonstration, messages were written by a member of the staff and handed to the Indian; he would transmit the message in his tribal dialect and the Indian on the other end would write it down in English. The text of messages as written and received are enclosed. The Indians do not have military terms in their dialect so it was necessary to give them a few minutes, before the demonstration, to improvise words for dive-bombing, anti-tank gun, etc.

3. Mr. Johnston stated that the Navajo is the only tribe in the United States that has not been infested with German students during the past twenty years. These Germans, studying the various tribal dialects under the guise of art students, anthropologists, etc., have undoubtedly attained a good working knowledge of all tribal dialects except Navajo. For this reason the Navajo is the only tribe available offering complete security for the type of work under consideration. It is noted in Mr. Johnston's article (enclosed) that the Navajo is the largest tribe but the lowest in literacy. He stated, however, that 1,000—if that many be needed—could be found with the necessary qualifications. It should also be noted that the Navajo tribal dialect is completely unintelligible to all other tribes and all other people, with the possible exception of as many as 28 Americans who have made a study of the dialect. This dialect is thus equivalent to a secret code to the enemy, and admirably suited for rapid, secure communication.

4. It is therefore recommended that an effort be made to enlist 200 Navajo Indians for this force. In addition to linguistic qualifications in English and their tribal dialect they should have the physical qualifications necessary for messengers.

CLAYTON B. VOGEL

Copy to CG, AFAF

Item III

2335 Norwalk Avenue
Los Angeles, California
September 14, 1942

The Commandant,
United States Marine Corps,
Washington, D. C.

Dear Sir:
I desire enlistment in the Marine Corps Reserve, Class 5-B, Specialist, to serve in the capacity of training and direction of

Navajo Indian personnel for communication, and to perform duty with them both inside and outside the limits of continental United States; with non-commissioned rank commensurate with duties assigned.

Your authority for my induction into the service is requested. The basis for this request is as follows:

Twenty-two years of residence among the Navajo Indians, starting when I was four years of age, enabled me to become fluent in the language of this tribe. At the age of nine, I acted as interpreter for President Theodore Roosevelt at the White House; and, subsequently, on many occasions, as court interpreter in Arizona. Since establishing my residence here, I have continued my use of the language through frequent visits to the reservation, and lecture work (see enclosed circulars).

Last February, it occurred to me that the Navajo language might be ideally suited to use by the Marine Corps for code in oral communication. I presented this idea to Lieutenant Colonel (then Major) J. E. Jones, Force Communication Officer at Camp Elliott, who agreed the plan was worth considering. I offered to make a search in Los Angeles for enough Navajos to permit a practical demonstration, and Colonel Jones accepted my offer. Two days after my return to this city, I received a letter from him, stating that General Vogel was interested, and requesting further information. A copy of his letter, and the report I prepared in compliance therewith, are enclosed.

On February 27th, I arrived at Camp Elliott with four Navajos; a fifth had been located in the Naval service at San Diego, and brought to Camp Elliott. The following morning at 8:15, Colonel Jones gave me six typical messages used in military operations, and asked me to report to Divisional Headquarters at nine o'clock for the demonstration. These messages contained many terms for which no equivalents exist in the Navajo language, and we had only a short time to devise such terms.

The demonstration was held as scheduled, in the presence of General Clayton B. Vogel and his staff. Its results and the General's verdict are summarized in the communication sent by him to your office on March 5th.

Recently, I made a trip to San Diego for the purpose of learning what progress had been made in utilizing the Navajo language for communications. Colonel Jones told me that the plan had been tried out with a limited number of Indians, had proved highly successful, and that he had requested authority to enlist additional personnel. I inquired if, in his opinion, my services could be utilized in the training of Navajos. His reply was a decided affirmative. He suggested that I contact the recruiting officer here, bearing in mind that I would need authorization to serve both inside and outside continental United States with the Indians.

Because of my great desire to be of service in the foregoing capacity, and to get started in this work at the earliest possible moment, I am applying for enlistment in the Marine Corps rather than for a commission, which would entail more time and uncertainty. As a further means of saving time, I have taken my physical examination at the local recruiting office, the results of which are shown on the enclosed application.

I have taken the liberty to explain in some detail the basis upon which I request favorable action from your office. I have marked the application "urgent" at the suggestion of the local recruiting officer, since my understanding of Navajo psychology would make me of value in the immediate future during recruiting of the new Indian personnel.

Very truly yours,

Philip Johnston

Item IV

PROCUREMENT OF NAVAJO PERSONNEL FOR COMMUNICATION DUTY

Part One

About the middle of September, 1942, a program of recruiting Navajo Indians qualified for duty as Communication Personnel was begun, with headquarters at Fort Wingate, New Mexico. Authority had been granted by the Commandant to recruit 200 for this purpose; but up to the first of the year only some 50 had been enlisted. The recent discontinuance of recruiting of all personnel for the armed forces, except those men which are 17 years of age, has brought to a halt the recruiting of Navajo Indians. This has occurred at a time of imperative need for such personnel to fill the requirements of the Commanding General, First Marine Division, as outlined by him after a test of Navajos now in service had shown the value of their language for transmitting confidential messages. Under the foregoing circumstances, plans for bringing into the

Marine Corps a sufficient complement of Navajos may well be considered.

Although the Navajo tribe numbers about 50,000, the percentage of illiteracy is high, and men whose education has been sufficient to enable them to master the technique of translating military messages into their native tongue are not numerous. The scarcity of such individuals has increased by the induction and enlistment of more than a thousand Navajos into various branches of the armed forces, chiefly the army. Consequently, efforts to procure a sufficient number for communication duty will entail an intensive canvass of schools attended by members of this tribe, a scrutiny of selective service registration rolls, and a diligent search for qualified individuals both on the reservation, and in adjacent towns where many have found employment.

Experience has shown that recruiting activities carried on from one central point, such as Fort Wingate, involves much lost motion and costly delay. This is particularly true if these headquarters are used as a focal point for contacting all portions of the reservation, which is equal to the state of West Virginia. It has been the practice of recruiting parties to make tours through different sections, generally planned to include the eastern or western half of the reservation, and often requiring five or six hundred miles of travel. The first visit to a given district accomplishes little more than the laying of groundwork for future enlistments. Those who are favorably impressed usually require from one to three weeks' time to wind up their affairs, say "goodbye" to their friends, and leave their homeland for an indefinite period. A second tour over the same territory is necessary for the purpose of gathering up those men who have decided to enlist. With headquarters in Fort Wingate, this means that a group of Navajos from Tuba City must be transported about three hundred miles to the recruiting office to be "written up" and sent to the Marine Corps Base at San Diego, stopping en route at Phoenix to be sworn in by the recruiting officer. In some cases, when transportation orders had become exhausted at the branch recruiting office, recruits were directed to stand by until more forms arrived. After an elapse of several days, they would become impatient and return to their homes, which were likely to be two or three hundred miles distant.

Procurement of a select group of Navajos could be put on an efficient basis by assigning this duty to a mobile unit in charge of a commissioned officer, assisted by one clerk and a Navajo Marine. A doctor would be desirable but not essential, as physical examinations could be arranged at various points on the reservation where government physicians are located. Such a unit, authorized to handle all details of enlistment where Navajos are found, would eliminate lost motion and delay which heretofore has resulted from remote control of recruiting on the Navajo Reservation.

Therefore, it is requested that permission be granted the Marine Corps to continue enlisting Navajos in accordance with the foregoing plan, until the original quota of 200 is filled.

Part Two

In the event that permission is not granted for enlistment of Navajos as outlined, an alternate plan for securing enough of such personnel should be considered, particularly if it proves necessary to work through selective service channels. Under such a program the mobile unit referred to would be equally essential, since it would speed up the process of locating and listing Navajos qualified for communication duty, which fall into three classes:

1. Men eligible for enlistment.
2. Men registered for selective service who are in Class 1A.
3. Men registered for selective service who are deferred because of dependents.

The first class mentioned, namely, men who are 17 years of age, may comprise excellent material if they have attended school at least seven years and have good records of scholarship. A complete survey of all schools on the reservation, and non-reservation schools, such as those located at Fort Wingate, Albuquerque, and Santa Fe, New Mexico, which are attended by Navajos, would disclose a list of potential enrollees for communication duty which might well prove to be among the best available. A careful check should be made on the scholarship of each individual to determine if he is qualified for the course. Then, too, those in the foregoing schools who are not more than a year below the enlistment age should be interviewed and appraised, with a view of possible enlistment after they have passed their seventeenth birthday.

The second class—men who have been placed in Class 1A by their draft boards—could be contacted by a mobile unit and informed of the opportunity offered by the Marine Corps for special duty as Communication Personnel. Those who desire to enter the service at once could do so through their draft boards according to procedure now followed. The recent act of Congress placing men 18 and 19 years of age under selective service has opened a reservoir of excellent material for communication work, since many of these individuals, now attending schools, would be well qualified.

The third category, those men who have been deferred by draft boards, is now well represented in the Navajo Communication School. Although it has been the policy of the Marine Corps not to accept for enlistment applicants who are married and have more than two children, this practice was set aside in the recent recruiting of Navajos, because of the scarcity of men qualified for communication duty. Allowances authorized for dependents have proved to be attractive for prospective recruits, since they represent incomes sufficient to maintain their families on the reservation. Under the present ruling, such men could enter the service by requesting their draft boards to place them in Class 1A, and induct them at once. The mobile recruiting unit could find these men, outline to them the attractive feature of specialized service in the Marine Corps, and direct them to the proper channel for induction.

As a means of facilitating a program of following up contacts made with prospective recruits, three separate card indices should be maintained, one for each of the foregoing classes. Data thus compiled would enable the mobile unit to carry on some of its business by correspondence, both with respective recruits, and with selective service boards through which they enter the service.

Item V

                    Field Signal Battalion
                    Training Center
                    Camp Pendleton, Oceanside, California

From: Philip Johnston, Staff Sergeant, U.S. Marine Corps
            Reserve
To: The Commandant, U.S. Marine Corps
Via: The Commanding Officer, Field Signal Battalion
            The Commanding General, Camp Pendleton
            The Commanding General, Fleet Marine Force San
            Diego Area
Subject: Navajo Indians, assignment of
Reference: 1535-110 AO-273 ma 1tr. from CMG to CG, First
            Marine Amphibious Corps, dated 16 April 1943

1. It has been proposed to recruit and train Navajo Personnel for "talkers" in the Marine Corps in sufficient numbers to assign 82 to each division. Since the Navajo program was started in May, 1942, a total of 163 have been enlisted, and given a special course of training

to qualify them for this service. The disposition of these men has been as follows:

Now overseas	67
Retained as instructors	5
Failed	24
In school	59
Standing by	8
Total	163

2. At the present time, procurement of Navajo personnel is falling much below the goal of 25 men per month as authorized in above reference, and prospects for obtaining educated Navajos at this rate appear to be negative. The principal reason for this scarcity is the fact that a large number of educated Navajos who are suitable for CP duties makes it apparent that the most effective use of the number available could be accomplished through a pool, unattached, from which assignments could be made as need arises for their services.

3. It is therefore recommended that a skeleton crew of Navajo "talkers" consisting of six to eight men be attached to each Marine Corps division to participate in tactical problems, and that the balance of Navajo personnel be assigned to a training center in the South Pacific Area. Allocations would be made from this pool to divisions about to enter a combat zone in which voice radio communication in the Navajo language would be an essential feature of contemplated operations.

4. It is further recommended that the South Pacific Navajo Training Center be placed in charge of Staff Sergeant Philip Johnston, and that the Navajo School, Training Center, Camp Pendleton, be placed under the supervision of an officer or non-commissioned officer who is qualified by experience in school work to handle this project.

Philip Johnston

Item VI

Office of the Commanding General
Second Marine Division, Fleet Marine Force in the Field
15 May 1943

From:	CG
To:	CG, FMAC
Subject:	Navajo Indians

References: (a) CG, FMAC ltr to CG, 2d MarDiv 1536-140 (o-369), 4588, dated 5 May 43.
(b) CMC Restricted Serial 46381 of 16 April 1943.

1. In compliance with the reference (a) the following report on the Navajo Indians assigned this Division is submitted:
   (a) In their primary billets as "talkers" they have functioned very well, handling traffic rapidly and accurately.
   (b) When not employed as "talkers," some of the Navajos have been used as message center men, and some as radio operators. They have functioned satisfactorily in both capacities.
   (c) As general duty Marines they have, in general, been excellent, showing above average willingness to work at any job assigned them.

2. It is recommended that the program of supplying Navajo Indians trained as "talkers" to Fleet Marine Force units be continued.

3. It is felt that allowances as outlined in reference (b) are dequate.

Julian C. Smith

Item VII

Headquarters,
First Marine Amphibious Corps, in the Field
22 June 1943

From: The Commanding General
To: The Commandant, U.S. Marine Corps
Subject: Navajo Indians
Reference: (a) CMC restricted serial 46381 or April 16, 1943.
Enclosure: (A) Copy ltr from SigCo, FMAC to CG, FMAC, dated 7 May 43.
           (B) Copy ltr from 1st MarParaRgt to CG, FMAC, dated 10 May 43.
           (C) Copy ltr from 1st MarDiv to CG, FMAC, dated 10 May 43.
           (D) Copy ltr from CG, 2nd MarDiv to CG, FMAC, dated 15 May 43.

1. As the enclosures indicate, it is considered very desirable to continue enlisting Navajo Indians for duty in the Marine Corps as Communication personnel.

2. The primary duties of these men should be that of "talkers" for transmitting messages in their own language over telephone circuits, as well as over radio circuits. Their secondary duties should be that of message center personnel (messengers). This designation will not limit their usefulness to the Marine Corps, however, as they have shown remarkable aptitude in the performance as general duty Marines.

3. The recommendation made by the 1st Marine Division as indicated in reference (a) is considered a minimum distribution. The following table is a suggested distribution and is also believed to be minimum requirements:

2 per Infantry and artillery battalion
4 per Infantry and artillery regiment
4 per Engineer regiment
2 per Engineer battalion
8 per Pioneer battalion
4 per Amphibian tractor battalion
6 per special weapons battalion
6 per tank company
6 per scout company
8 per signal company
2 per parachute battalion
4 per parachute regiment
8 per raider battalion
6 per raider regiment
8 per corps signal battalion
8 per corps anti tank battalion
4 per corps 155m artillery battalion

A. F. Howard, by direction

Copy to: CG 1st MarDiv
CG 2d MarDiv
CG 3d MarDiv
CO 1st ParaRegt
CO 1st RdrRegt
CO Corps SigBn

Item VIII

Field Signal Battalion
Training Center, Camp Pendleton
Oceanside, California

30 August 1943

From:	NCO in charge, Navajo Communication School	
To:	The Commandant, U.S. Marine Corps	
Via:	(1) The Commanding Officer, Field Signal Battalion	
	(2) The Commanding General, Training Center, Camp Pendleton	
	(3) The Commanding General, Fleet Marine Force, San Diego area	
Subject:	Navajo Indians	
References:	(a) 1535-110 A0273 Ma ltr from CMC to CO, First Marine Amphibious Corps, dated 16 April 1943.	
	(b) 1535-140 (0-486) 15/116jht ltr. from CG, First Marine Amphibious Corps to CMO, dated 22 June 1943.	

1. It has been proposed to recruit and train Navajo personnel for "talkers" in the Marine Corps in sufficient numbers to assign 100 to each division. Since the Navajo program was started in May, 1942, a total of 191 have been enlisted, and the disposition of these men has been as follows:

Finished course	67
Retained as instructors	5
Failed	27
Attending school	92

2. At the present time, procurement of Navajo personnel is falling much below the goal of 25 men per month as authorized in reference (a), and prospects for obtaining educated Navajos at this rate appear to be negative. The principal reason is that a large number have already been inducted into the army. This indicated shortage of Navajos who may be qualified for CP duties makes it apparent that the most effective use of the number available could be accomplished through a pool, unattached, from which assignments would be made as need arises for their services.

3. It is therefore recommended that a skeleton crew of qualified Navajo "talkers" be attached to each Marine Corps division to participate in tactical problems, and that the balance of Navajo personnel be assigned to a training center in the South Pacific Area. Allocations would be made from this pool to divisions about to enter a combat zone, in which voice radio communications would be an essential feature of contemplated operations. The advantages of such a plan are three-fold:

(a) Integration of Navajo personnel as one unit would overcome a tendency of detached groups to develop idiomatic usages of words and phrases which are variants from the primary instruction in military communication. This inclination has been observed among classes working concurrently in the Navajo School, and arises from the fact that the Navajo language must be greatly distorted when a message is transmitted verbatim from the English. Continued practice alone can insure the speed and accuracy essential to military operations, and collaboration of all personnel in such practice will promote uniformity and avoid possible confusion.

(b) Combat experiences of Navajo personnel, together with criticisms and suggestions from officers who have made use of Navajo communication in the combat areas will comprise invaluable data to be added to instruction procedure.

(c) The shortage of Navajo personnel can at least be partially offset by a plan of rationing, under which a division about to enter a combat area would be allocated a sufficient number of "talkers" from the pool to man all voice radio circuits in the lower echelons which may be in close contact with the enemy. This will eliminate the necessity for authenticating transmissions, and secure all traffic from enemy interception.

4. It is further recommended that the following steps be taken to accelerate the induction of Navajos qualified for communication duties:

(a) Request the superintendent of the Navajo Reservation to compile a list of qualified personnel available for induction who are now residing under his jurisdiction. This may be accomplished through cooperation of traders and principals of various reservation schools.

(b) Request that selective service authorities advise all draft boards in Arizona, New Mexico, and southern California of the special need for educated Navajos in the Marine Corps, in order that such personnel, now employed off the reservation in large numbers, may be assigned to this branch of the service.

Philip Johnston

BIBLIOGRAPHY

Books

Brookhauser, Frank, ed., *This Was Your War,* New York: Doubleday, 1960.

Link, Martin A., ed., *Navajo—A Century of Progress 1868-1968,* Window Rock, Arizona: Navajo Tribe, 1968.

Newcomb, Richard F., *Iwo Jima,* San Francisco: Holt, Rinehart and Winston, 1965.

Schultz, Joy, *The West Still Lives,* Dallas: Heritage Press, 1970.

Toland, John, *The Rising Sun,* New York: Random House, 1970.

Tregaskis, Richard, *Guadalcanal Diary,* New York: Random House, 1943.

Underhill, Ruth, *Here Come the Navajo,* New York: Haskell Press, 1953.

Newspapers

Coconino Sun (Flagstaff), March 5, 1943.

Gallup (NM) *Independent,* September 2, 1969.

San Diego Union, September 18, 1945.

Magazines and Other Periodicals

From Our Heritage, July, 1971: Kelly, T. O., "Navajo Talkers Confused the Japanese . . . and Sometimes the Marines."

Headquarters Bulletin, September, 1944: "Red Man Hits the War Path."

The Leatherneck, vol. 31-A, March, 1948: "Indian War Call."

Look Magazine, June 2, 1970: Hedgepath, William, "Timeless People, Changing Earth."

Marine Corps Chevron, January 23, 1943: "Navajos Readying to Going Tough for Japanazis."

Marine Corps Gazette, September, 1945: Marder, Murrey (Mt. Sgt.), "Navajo Code Talkers."

National Geographic, vol. 142, no. 6, December, 1972: Looney, Ralph and Dale, Bruce, "The Navajo Nation Looks Ahead."

AFTERWORD

After almost twenty years of seeing *The Navajo Code Talkers* continuously available and in print, it is gratifying to know that this work, written entirely from primary sources—the first to pull together all the major facts concerning the code talkers project—has attracted national interest.

To my great satisfaction, Lieutenant General Seizo Arisue, Chief of Intelligence in Japan during World War II, certified the fact the enemy was never able to break the code.

Also, in a way, writing this book was a labor of love, for I felt that the world should know about the significant contribution these brave native Americans made in this critical conflict. Someone has said, use of the Navajo code was "the best-kept secret of the war." Now it is surely known.